Fine Lines

WALKING THE LABYRINTH OF GRIEF AND LOSS

KATHY SWAAR

Cover and interior illustrations copyright © 2015, Kathryn Coneway. To contact Kathryn or see more of her work, go to her website at www.kathrynconeway.com. Cover design by Susanne Clark (www.creativeblueprintdesign.com).

ISBN 978-1-7358079-0-4

CONTENTS

Introduction 5

Part I   Letting Go **11**

1. There is a fine line between the thrill of victory and the
agony of defeat. *Invitation: Start where you are.* 13

2. There is a fine line between doing everything you can
and not doing nearly enough. *Invitation: Let go of expectations.* 19

3. There is a fine line between giving up and giving in.
Invitation: Let go of assumptions. 25

4. There is a fine line between a line in the sand and a gaping,
unbridgeable chasm. *Invitation: Let go of what you can't control.* 33

Part II   Twists and Turns **39**

5. There is a fine line between faith and doubt.
Invitation: Befriend unknowing. 41

6. There is a fine line between conscientious and
compulsive. *Invitation: Move beyond your default setting.* 49

7. There is a fine line between compliment and criticism.
Invitation: Honor the embodied. 57

8. There is a fine line between having everything you need
and having too much stuff. *Invitation: Trust your worth.* 65

Part III   Moving the Chairs **73**

9. There is a fine line between solitude and heartbreaking,
soul-crushing loneliness. *Invitation: Come home to you.* 75

10. There is a fine line between a few bumps and bruises and
a stab in the heart. *Invitation: Speak with care.* 85

11. There is a fine line between the leading edge of progress and the ragged edge of disaster. *Invitation: Look beyond either/or.* 93

12. There is a fine line between knowing about something and having it etched into your life and experience. *Invitation: Name your truth.* 103

Part IV   Takeaways **113**

13. There is a fine line between worn and worn out. *Invitation: Be real.* 115

14. There is a fine line between "I've never done it that way before!" and "Sure. Why not?" *Invitation: Do new things in new ways.* 123

15. There is a fine line between getting there and being there. *Invitation: Be present.* 131

16. There's a fine line between pondering and sheer avoidance. *Invitation: It is what it is. Embrace it.* 139

Afterword 149

"Tribal Talk," original poem by William D. Swaar 151

Acknowledgments 153

About the Author 157

INTRODUCTION

For the last five years of his life, my husband constantly badgered me—in the nicest possible way, of course—about when I was going to quit my day job and write. I always responded—in the nicest possible way, of course—by reminding him that we needed my day job to help support his farming habit, so that wasn't going to happen any time soon.

And then he was gone.

Suddenly, unexpectedly, less than three months after our first inkling there was something really wrong.

Bill's death shattered both my heart and the circumstances of my life, creating a series of fine lines resembling the circular splintering of safety glass hit with a hammer or baseball bat. Everything changed. The day job was no more. I no longer knew who I was, what to do, or how to be.

Bound by my own self-imposed *shoulds, oughts, can'ts,* and *musts,* along with the constraints of a culture that doesn't want to talk about grief—and doesn't know how—I had no place to put all that overwhelming emotion, no idea how to unpack all the baggage around what I thought I knew about it and the shape and form my grief actually took. And the one person I would have turned to in the face of trauma of that magnitude—the one who held my heart, always had my back, the one I could tell anything—was the one who was gone.

Not knowing what else to do—and to fill all those hours I now spent home alone—I picked up my pen and Julia Cameron's *The Right to Write* and started working my way through it. The prompt for the chapter on voice instructed us to "time-travel back along your own life—your narrative time line—and stop at a time or an episode that is emotionally charged for you. You are then asked to scoop this 'cup' of time from your life and write about it."[1] It included a list of ten examples. Item four—"my greatest loss"—jumped off the page and screamed my name.

But I wasn't ready to go there yet. I slammed the book shut, put it back on the shelf, and grabbed one I knew would not require me to write anything: Tolkien's *The Lord of the Rings.*

Yet I couldn't stop thinking about it—and about Bill and what he always wanted me to do. So a month later, I got it back down and started writing again. That prompt turned out to be just enough to give me permission to pour all the things I didn't think I was allowed to feel, think, or say—all the messy details of life without the one I

---

1 Julia Cameron, *The Right to Write: An Invitation and Initiation into the Writing Life* (New York: Jeremy P. Tarcher/Putnam, 1998), 160.

loved most—out onto the page. And in the writing of the fine lines of my grief, this book was conceived.

But I struggled with how to organize the chapters. Because of grief's nonlinear nature and its stubborn resistance to any sort of categorizing and quantifying, it wasn't possible to put the chapters in truly chronological order. When I discussed this in a session with my spiritual director, Trudy stopped me mid-sentence and asked if she could share an image she'd received while I was speaking. It was the labyrinth. She graciously sent me home with her Chartres hand labyrinth to use and sit with until our next visit, to see if the labyrinth theme held.

It did.

A clear order for the chapters emerged, divided into four sections—as is the Chartres labyrinth—and mirroring the process and experience of walking the labyrinth as spiritual practice: letting go, navigating the twists and turns, finding your own pace/path to the center, and returning.

Walking the labyrinth of grief and loss requires letting go of what was in order to face what is and remain open to what may be. It is full of ins and outs, twists and turns. Unlike my original perception of them—that life on one side of those fine lines was livable, and on the other side it was not—the fine lines of loss are not either/or. They are interconnected, spiraling out and back on each other, and together form one continuous path. While grief is universal, each of us experiences it uniquely; we have to make our own way, at our own pace. And all along the way, even in the wreckage of our lives, the broken shards, the bits and pieces, there are invitations, gifts and graces, knowledge and insight.

Using personal narrative, pastoral reflection, and prayers, each chapter in this book explores one of the fine lines of grief I encountered and the invitation nestled within that fine line.

A note on the prayers. One of the biggest challenges of Bill's stunning diagnosis and rapid decline and death was the fact that everything happened so fast: I had no time to adequately process it. In shock, numb, I simply could not pray in the traditional sense. I did not have the words. They have finally come, and I have included a prayer at the end of each chapter. If you too are struggling to pray and can't find the words, use mine.

The invitations included for each chapter offer a glimpse beyond the pain of the immediate circumstance and the opportunity to make connections of your own along the way: to your truest self, to others, and to the Holy.

This book is not a how-to. It cannot fix or remove pain.

Instead, it companions.

Henri Nouwen says, "The friend who can be silent with us in a moment of despair or confusion, who can stay with us in an hour of grief and bereavement, who can tolerate not knowing, not curing, not healing and face with us the reality of our powerlessness, that is a friend who cares."[2]

---

2 Henri Nouwen, *Out of Solitude: Three Meditations on the Christian Life* (Notre Dame, IN: Ave Maria Press, 2004), 38.

Consider this book the literary equivalent of that friend. It will sit with you, hold space for your tears, pray when you can't. It will not offer answers or solutions, because grief isn't a problem or question; it is simply part of being human. Instead, it will be with you, and by its presence, give you permission to be: who you are, where you are, how you are.

Part I

LETTING GO

*T*he labyrinth walk is a pilgrimage of invitation. At every step along the way, we find opportunities to start, to pause, to revisit, to notice, to ponder, to learn, and ultimately to take what we experience with us into the wider world and the rest of our lives. In her first encounter with the pattern, labyrinth pioneer Lauren Artress studied with psychologist, scholar, and author Dr. Jean Houston, "who described a powerful spiritual tool whose path would lead each of us to our own center."[3]

My experience of grief has mirrored and embodied all of that. The sudden, unexpected death of my husband of forty-one years and 361 days—my soulmate and best friend—was both beginning and end. It changed my identity in multiple ways, and I had to dis-

---

3 Lauren Artress, *Walking a Sacred Path: Rediscovering the Labyrinth as a Spiritual Practice* (New York: Riverhead Books, 2006), 2.

cern all over again who I was now and where I fit in the world. Coming to terms with that loss has been like walking the labyrinth, full of stops and starts, twists and turns, taking me to the center of myself and back out, over and over again.

Those who walk the labyrinth as a spiritual practice often begin by consciously and intentionally quieting and emptying the mind as they follow the path. Likewise, grieving is an ongoing process of releasing, of letting go: letting go of what was, what isn't, what will now never be; letting go of assumptions, expectations, things we can't control, and what no longer fits or serves; and letting go of what confuses or distracts in order to be fully present to what is and open to what may be.

Chapter 1

THERE IS A FINE LINE BETWEEN THE THRILL OF VICTORY AND THE AGONY OF DEFEAT.

Invitation: Start where you are.

I am a sports junkie. It is both hardwired into my DNA and anchored in my experience. My earliest memories are of sitting on my dad's lap watching boxing and baseball on Friday nights and Saturday and Sunday afternoons. Littered across my family tree, you'll find sports promoters, semi-pro and professional athletes, coaches, officials, and a plethora of "almost-made-its." I cut my teeth on ABC's *Wide World of Sports*, enthralled by the trumpet fanfare, the announcer's assurance that we would see it all, "from the thrill of victory to the agony of defeat," and the stunning video footage of both that started every show.

From 2014 on, that iconic intro has defined my life.

The last week of January 2014 found my husband, Bill, and I at Walt Disney World with our kids and half of our grandkids. We'd planned the trip for nearly a year, and when we arrived, we each had lofty expectations of what that vacation would be like. It had been two years and three weeks since we'd all been together, and planning for a trip that juggled nine people living in three states, plus multiple jobs and schedules that included trying not to run afoul of the polity and policies of two congregations, the federal government, and three school systems made for multiple opportunities along the way for plans to go very, very wrong. But they did not. It was everything all of us expected it to be, and more. It was *perfect*. We returned home in mid-February on an emotional high. Life was good—so, so good—and I could not imagine how it could get much better.

The thrill of victory, indeed.

One month later, our world was ripped apart by one vague symptom that became two small words—*brain tumors*—that ultimately turned out to be a death sentence. In the blink of an eye, our lives became the second half of the *Wide World of Sports* intro, where the ski jumper careens out of control and crashes in the snow. The instant the ER physician uttered those two words, life as we had known it turned to ashes around us.

It happens. One minute everything is fine; the next it is not. The phone rings. You get a text. Someone in uniform comes to the door. The chaplain meets you in the hospital hallway. There's a "Breaking News" report. A cough turns into a coma. You're doing the most glorious or innocuous of things, and tragedy unfolds right in front of you.

Even though I was a pastor at the time of my husband's diagnosis and death, nothing in my theological training or decades of pastoral ministry prepared me for the moment it happened to me—when that fine line was crossed, and life went from normal to unthinkable in an instant.

My shell-shocked brain, trying to comprehend the incomprehensible, kept insisting, "This can't be happening. It isn't real." I fully expected to wake up the next morning and find it was all just a bad dream and everything was fine.

It wasn't.

Over the next ten days, the progression of consultations, appointments, and tests brought the severity of my husband's illness into stunningly clear focus.

It was real, it was terminal, and it was terrifying.

My thoughts moved from denial to trying to pinpoint the cause, wondering what we shouldn't have done or could have done to prevent this. I scrutinized every detail of our lives, looking for answers to all those *how*, *why*, and *what if* questions.

In our case, there were none.

It seemed so important at the time, but all the incessant questioning did was suck precious time and emotional energy away from the one thing that mattered most: being fully present during the few fleeting days we had left when my husband was cognizant and responsive.

I wanted to go back, redo, undo.

That isn't within our purview, nor can we fully envision or craft what the future will entail.

All we have is now.

Start there. Whether disaster is looming, you're in the midst of it, or you're trying to recover from it, start where you are, how you are—not how you wish things were, how you think you should be, or how the world expects you to be.

Let go of what was, what is not now, and what will never be. Face what is. Name it. Feel it. Sit with it. Pay attention to what it tells you.

I didn't, and I should have.

Swept up in caring for Bill during the rapid progression of his glioblastoma, I doggedly put one foot in front of the other, shoving the emotions aside and telling myself I didn't have time to fall apart. I was afraid if I allowed myself to fully experience everything I was feeling, I would be overwhelmed, consumed, rendered nonfunctional. I would never be able to get all that toothpaste back into the tube.

In fact, the opposite is true.

We learn—gain wisdom—through experience, and when we fail to allow ourselves to experience grief and loss—when we avoid or deny—we never learn how to find our way or help others do so. Any hope of picking up the pieces of our life and moving toward wholeness requires that we first admit our life has been shattered. So wherever you are, however you are, name and own how you feel, even if how you feel is horrible.

Doing this will not diminish you, nor is it a sign of incompetence or weakness. It is, according to Brené Brown, an act of courage and bravery. In her book *The Gifts of Imperfection*, Brown says, "Speaking honestly and openly about who we are, about what we're feeling, and about our experiences (good and bad) is the definition of courage."[4] Start where you are. Be present, and face and name what is.

Here am I.

Isaiah 6:8 NIV

---

4 Brené Brown, *The Gifts of Imperfection: Let Go of Who You Think You're Supposed to Be and Embrace Who You Are* (Center City, MN: Hazelden Publishing, 2010), 12–13.

A Prayer for Here

Here I am, Holy One.
And it's not a pretty place.
Not where I want to be,
not at all where I think I should be.

I don't feel strong enough, faith-full enough, brave enough,
or courageous enough to walk this labyrinth of loss.

What I'm full of is fear, worry, sorrow, questions.
My thoughts mirror Isaiah's: "Woe is me! I am ruined!"
Like Moses, I wonder, "Why me? Why us? Why now?"
I ask, like Gideon, "If you are indeed with us, Lord,
why has all this happened?"

And all I hear is silence.

So I cling, Sacred Presence, to the answers you
gave my ancestors in faith:
"I Am.
I am here.
I will go with you."
I am not where I want to be, Holy One, but here I am.
Where are you?

Chapter 2

THERE IS A FINE LINE BETWEEN DOING EVERYTHING YOU CAN AND NOT DOING NEARLY ENOUGH.

Invitation: Let go of expectations.

There is ingrained in many of us a deep-seated conviction that it—*everything*—is all up to us. A Rumpelstiltskin-esque expectation that we are obligated to take the myriad piles of straw that make up our lives and somehow turn them into gold, that we must be all things to all people at all times and in all places and do it all perfectly.

There is a multitude of reasons for this, unique to each one of us. In my case, I was a product of my environment. A combination of global and personal events snowballed into one another, making my parents' lives difficult at times. At an early age, I internalized the idea that I needed to do everything in my power to make things as perfect as possible so I didn't add to the difficulties. That meant following both the spirit and the letter of the law. It meant trying to anticipate every circumstance and need and reacting accordingly in order to prevent or defuse problems. It meant not calling attention to myself in any manner, especially in a negative way. I had to do it all and do it all right the first time. This became one of my standard operating procedures, bleeding over into everything I turned my hand to, the Organizational Perfectionist in my head constantly reminding me every time I didn't measure up, and how.

When it came to Bill's illness, this complicated the already stressful reality exponentially. With a terminal diagnosis, everything takes on deeper significance. It's all a matter of life and death; everything feels monumental. Like Vince Vaughn's character, Eddie, in the movie *Mr. & Mrs. Smith*, I spent every moment on high alert, trying to plan ahead for every possible circumstance and need, constantly searching for ways to make the oh-so-short amount of time we had left as good and life-giving as it could be.

This meant making sure Bill was bathed and dressed in clean clothes and had a freshly made bed—a process it was often necessary to repeat multiple times a day; following the medication schedule to the minute so there were no issues with discomfort or seizures and so function was as good as it could be; and cooking his favorite foods while he still enjoyed eating. It meant finding a TV show or movie for him to watch because he could do little else, which also entailed a crash course in PlayStation 101 for me, since Bill could no longer explain how to operate it, nor did he have enough fine motor skills left to use the controls himself. It meant running interference with the endless stream of visitors and phone callers, which included ensuring he had an opportunity to speak with the people he needed and wanted to converse with, protecting him from trying to do too much in too short a time, shielding him as much as possible from worry and stress, and trying to find a polite way to say no when he wasn't up for company or conversation (something he was not always aware of). It meant curbing the dog so her barking didn't disturb Bill's rest or terrorize those who came to see him, coordinating the doctors' and nurses' visits, and doing what was necessary to keep the farm running. And, most importantly, it meant spending every second I could at his side—all while doing all those other unthinkable things that were also on the landscape: disability paperwork, phone calls to Social Security, helping him craft the resignation letter to his congregation, and discussing funeral arrangements with him and our denominational staff.

But the light speed at which Bill's level of function declined blanketed every interaction in uncertainty. By the time we knew what was wrong, his cognitive abilities were already limited, making his responses often unreliable or incomprehensible. It was too late for any meaningful conversation about what was happening to him and to us and how to make our way through it.

I did my best to figure it out on my own. I thought. I rethought. I analyzed. I second-guessed. I examined and reexamined what I was doing, weighing which side of that fine line between enough and not enough I was on, haunted by how quickly time was running out.

I did everything I could, but I wanted to do so *much more.*

I wanted to do it all.

I wanted to fix it.

And when I couldn't—when doing everything wasn't going to change anything—it crushed me.

In Mark 6:30–44, we find Mark's record of Jesus feeding the five thousand. The disciples were worried—as they often were—about many things. The hour was late, and they pressed Jesus to call it a day, to dismiss the crowd so people could make their way to nearby towns and villages and get something to eat. Jesus turned the tables on them, telling the disciples to feed the multitude themselves. Even pooling their resources, they fell far, far short of having enough cash to purchase food for that many, and between them they had but five loaves of bread and two fish—at which point Jesus said, basically, "Give me what you have."

That's what I'd done. For each moment of each of those days, to the best of my ability at the time, I gave what I had.

Was it sufficient?

I didn't think so.

But whether it felt like I had done enough or not was not the issue. The divine economy functions at levels and in ways that are beyond our human understanding and awareness. How I measured what I'd done—what I'd considered to be little, nothing, or inconsequential any way I sliced it in the face of Bill's looming death—was not what mattered. What mattered was that I had done what I could—done my best and gave what I had—and as best I could, had released my husband to God's care.

We finite, human creatures cannot, by ourselves, in our own strength, make enough, do enough, be enough. We can't do it all. And that's not our job. It is the Holy One who takes what we have—

what we can do and are willing to give—and does the multiplication that creates "enough," and in many cases much, much more.

All you can do is what you can.

Let go of your (and everyone else's) expectations, which, according to Anne Lamott and the Twelve Steps community, are just "resentments under construction" anyway. Don't get caught up in what everyone else thinks ought to be done, and don't *should* all over yourself. Do what you can, ask for help when you can't, and leave the rest in God's hands.

My grace is sufficient.

2 Corinthians 12:9 NIV

A Quantitative Prayer

The list is long, Holy One. So long.
There are so many things to manage and tend,
each day a marathon of Must-Dos, all
meant to maintain quality of life.

Yet little helps.

Regardless of the quantity of things done,
quality is hard to come by in this terminal, invalid existence.
Function declines at light speed,
our days defined by "cannot" and "do not."

This shift from soulmate and confidant to
caregiver and keeper is soul searing.
The losses pile up like the crumpled cars of a train wreck,
the one I love disappearing before my eyes.

Remind me again, Holy One,
that doing what I can is enough,
that the only "do nots" that truly matter are yours:
"Do not worry. Do not be afraid."

Chapter 3

THERE IS A FINE LINE BETWEEN GIVING UP AND GIVING IN.

Invitation: Let go of assumptions.

*W*hen Bill died, just four days shy of our forty-second wedding anniversary, I was forced to give up a lifetime's worth of hopes, dreams, and plans. As the next youngest in his family of origin—more than a decade younger than his older siblings—all kinds of other things I, we, and everyone else assumed would happen or he would do disappeared when he took his last breath.

We were already plotting our retirement timetable and strategy. We never got that far. We had thought about—and discussed at length—our seventy-fifth wedding anniversary celebration because we had married young enough to have a chance of marking that milestone and wanted to do it meaningfully and well. Except now, of course, we won't. We didn't even make it to fifty. There will be no growing old together. No days filled with the pursuit of our many shared interests. No long, lingering dinners. No traveling to our ancestors' homelands. No celebrating together the graduations and engagements and marriages of our grandchildren or the births of our great-grandchildren.

There were times in those early days of raw grief when the idea of giving up on everything else—not doing anything about anything, for any reason—was extremely attractive. I truly didn't know at that point whether I could survive without him or if I even wanted to try.

Nothing seemed to matter anyway. Even when I was busy doing things, the sensation of being utterly lost and abandoned permeated everything I turned my hand to, draping each task in a mantle of meaninglessness.

The simplest of things were monumental challenges. Just getting up and getting dressed was exhausting. The thought of leaving the house filled me with dread. What if I started sobbing in the grocery store produce aisle or at the attorney's office or at the post office or at the gas station and couldn't stop? I was afraid both of making a spectacle of myself and of making others uncomfortable or suspect of my mental health.

Staying home was no better. Rattling around in that huge house with nothing to keep me company but my questions and my tears was sheer agony.

I tried to do what I assumed I was supposed to: stay strong, keep trying, keep going, never give up, never give in.

But even when I told myself I would not give in, I did. I gave in a hundred times a day over a hundred different things. I gave in to the tears, the anger, the frustration, the unfairness, the weariness, the confusion, the fear—all of it.

What I'd been told bore no resemblance to what my reality turned out to be. Both culture and what I saw, heard, and learned in my formative years—I was raised by parents of the "greatest generation"—insisted that neither giving up nor giving in was acceptable. Giving in was regarded as weakness, a personality flaw, a moral failure, as was any public expression of emotion, particularly tender emotions like tears—"going to pieces," as it was cryptically phrased in my family of origin.

Giving up was even worse, a sure sign of laziness or incompetence or both, and the shame associated with that was palpable. In my family, you didn't quit; it wasn't allowed. You didn't even stop to rest. You just kept going, kept working, until whatever was in front of you was completed, and then you moved on to the next thing on the list.

But grief is not a task to be accomplished or a project to finish. It is part of life, something you become acquainted with, come to terms with, live into.

I was on one side of that fine line, and the rest of the world was on the opposite side, going all Jim Valvano on me: "Don't give up. Don't ever give up!" My most recent lived experience told me one thing: owning and living into my new reality required me, at times, to give in, to let go. Everything and everyone else screamed the exact opposite.

Don't get me wrong. I deeply admire the former North Carolina State basketball coach and the courage he displayed during his cancer battle. I was watching the ESPYs on the March night in 1993 when he gave the speech that included those words, and I have no doubt that was truth for him. When I initially heard it, I found it inspirational myself. But experience has taught me those words are not always true for everyone all the time. There were times when they weren't true for me.

Culture says never give up—keep trying, pushing through, soldiering on.

Sometimes you just can't.

You can't drag yourself out of bed. Can't stop crying. Can't cook a meal. Can't remember if you brushed your hair or teeth. You can't answer one more phone call. Can't write one more thank-you note. Can't empty one more drawer. Can't read yet another sympathy card. Can't face that "How are you?" question no one wants to hear the real answer to. Can't imagine leaving the house. Can't focus long enough to write a check or read the mail.

I had to give in. I had to stop trying to hold it all together, keep up appearances, fulfill all those expectations the Organizational Perfectionist in my head insisted were so important. I had to let the tears flow, whenever and wherever that was.

And I had to give up—to let go of doing—so I could be, rest, regroup.

It's okay to stop.

Doing something is not always better than doing nothing.

Stopping—even for just a moment or two—affords us the opportunity to breathe. To see where we are. To examine the terrain and get the lay of the land. To notice what's there and what isn't. To gauge how far and from whence we've come.

If we don't stop and still ourselves, we risk missing the Holy in our midst, the God who is present in all things—the lofty and the lowly, the miraculous and the mundane, in the best and the worst, in the organization and the chaos. There are times, as the author, artist, and pastor Jan Richardson says, when we need "[to shut up] long enough to notice God shuffling around in the daily events that make up our lives."[5]

It is a delicate dance along that fine line, a precise waltz of intention and discernment to figure out the appropriate response in each particular situation. Rather than the negative, or weakness, our culture labels giving up and giving in to be, they are, in fact, courageous acts of survival, of faith, of surrender. They are an offering—a sacrifice, which in its Latin roots has to do with making sacred. "The ability to rest," Joan Chittister says, "gives the world back to God for a while."[6]

When things aren't working, when you're overwhelmed with emotion, when it's a horrible day and there's nothing you can do about the horror of it all, give yourself permission to give up, give in, or stop completely, as you need to.

Take a break. Take several deep breaths. Close your eyes and soak in the silence. Grab your beverage of choice and sit and sip it. Go for a walk. Take a nap. Curl up with a book. Dig in the dirt. Watch your favorite TV show or movie. Snuggle with the cat or the dog. Voice a prayer or mantra. Ponder a section of scripture or poetry. Play your favorite music. Call a friend. Have some ice cream or a salad. Draw. Doodle. Write. Sew. Knit.

Or do nothing at all.

---

5 Jan L. Richardson, *In the Sanctuary of Women: A Companion for Reflection and Prayer* (Nashville: Upper Room Books, 2010), 194.

6 Sister Joan Chittister, "The Sabbath: Making Something New," Huff-Post, July 17, 2010, https://www.huffpost.com/entry/the-sabbath-making-someth_b_643716.

There will be time down the road to try again, to keep going, to lean into the pain, to continue to put one foot in front of the other until you make it to the center and back out again.

In returning and rest you shall be saved;
in quietness and in trust shall be your strength.
Isaiah 30:15 RSV

On Giving Up and Giving In

*Those words—giving up *and* giving in—sound so weaselly.*
So weak, so less than, so loser.
And that's how I was conditioned to feel about them.

Yet weakness is not condemned in your Word, Holy One.
It is embraced.
You offer blessing to, stand in solidarity with, and fiercely defend
those culture labels weak:
the poor, the poor in spirit, the persecuted, those who mourn.

To hear the Apostle Paul tell it, our weakness is the very doorway
through which your divine power enters and is made manifest in us.
But it's so hard to turn off those old scripts—
the ones full of judgment for every perceived fault or omission,
which giving up and giving in surely are, so we've been told.

The what-ifs, the if-onlys, are on auto play.
Along with all the shoulds, the ought-tos, the have-tos, the can'ts,
the might-have-beens, the should-have-beens.

Oh, God. I can't quit thinking about those.

Look upon me with compassion, Holy One.
Help me let go,
to lay it all down as an offering
on your altar of grace.

I give up, Divine Mercy. And I give in.
I surrender to your love, your grace, your presence, your peace.

Chapter 4

THERE IS A FINE LINE BETWEEN A LINE IN THE SAND AND A GAPING, UNBRIDGEABLE CHASM.

Invitation: Let go of what you can't control.

*P*ain and suffering, regardless of its root cause, is a great isolator, both for the afflicted and those most closely connected to them. For me, the isolation brought about by my husband's sudden illness and death became a highly accurate barometer for the health of my personal relationships.

It isn't just a cliché: when the unthinkable happens and renders you unable to participate in life as you previously had, you learn very quickly who your real friends and supporters are—and who they are not. Additionally, death has a nasty habit of shoving everything under the microscope and magnifying whatever is there—good and bad alike—a millionfold. If the ties that bound you together were strong, the relationship will likely hold, even in the face of massive upheaval. It's even possible the connection will deepen. But if things were rocky to begin with, the relationship will likely crumble under the added stress that traumatic events inevitably bring.

I knew there were people I could count on for anything I needed during our sojourn through the "valley of the shadow of death" (Ps. 23:4 RSV). They were there every step of the way and then some. They brought meals. They scrubbed my kitchen floor, loaded the dishwasher, took out the trash. They sat with Bill so I could run errands. They helped him bathe, get to and from the bathroom, and get in and out of bed. They changed the sheets, mowed the lawn, and weeded my flower beds. They removed doors and moved furniture to accommodate the walker, then the wheelchair, then the hospital bed. They tried valiantly (but unsuccessfully) to remove the bat—mammal, not baseball—from the basement. They sent flowers, wrote notes, called to check on us, prayed for us. They came to visit and brought movies to watch and treats to snack on. They listened while Bill tried to communicate, doing their best to try to understand him. They helped me get him up off the floor when he fell. There were nights when they stayed and slept on the couch next to the hospital bed in case he needed pain meds during the night so I had a chance to rest.

But anywhere fault lines already existed in relationships, cracks started forming immediately. Bill had always sought to be the negotiator and peacemaker. Even in situations where a complete resolution of differences was not possible, he could usually broker a truce that allowed those involved to agree to disagree and move on. The moment he was no longer able to do that, the divisions returned.

For a while, I entertained the fantasy that our circumstances— his terminal illness—might be the catalyst for finally securing the fault lines in those relationships, bringing some good out of this horrible situation, uncovering a silver lining in the clouds that overshadowed our existence and darkened our days.

It didn't happen. That fine line already crossed, the chasms deepened. Promises were made but not followed through on. Intentions were questioned, resentments refueled. Conversations became potential powder kegs.

I wanted—more than anything—to mend fences and bridge gaps. My heart already shattered, my deepest human connection gone, I wasn't sure I could survive the loss of even one more relationship. But there came a point when I realized this wasn't all mine to do and that if I kept trying, I was in danger of losing myself and any chance for (possibly, one day) reconciliation.

As Joan Chittister puts it in her book *Scarred by Struggle, Transformed by Hope,*

> there are times to let a thing go. There is a time to put a thing down, however unresolved, however baffling, however wrong, however unjust it may be. There are some things in life that cannot be changed, no matter how intent we are to change them. There is a time to let surrender take over so that the past does not consume the present, so that new life can come, so that joy has a chance to surprise us again.[7]

Our heart's cry, when things in our lives are difficult or amiss, whether or not we acknowledge or name it as such, is for healing,

---

7 Joan D. Chittister, *Scarred by Struggle, Transformed by Hope* (Grand Rapids, MI: Eerdmans, 2003), 60.

for restoration. We want to stop the pain, to mend that gaping hole in our heart where the very life is hemorrhaging out of us. It isn't always possible to do that in the time frame or the manner we envision or desire, and as Chittister points out, in some instances it's not possible at all.

There are things over which we have no control.

I am only half of the equation in any given relationship. I cannot make grown-up, adult people do things they don't want to do. I cannot change someone else's mind, heart, or behavior if they don't see the need for it or have any desire to change. It isn't possible for me to undo or rearrange the past. I cannot alter others' perceptions and reasoning.

Likewise, the rest of the world is not responsible for, nor do they get to dictate, who I am, how I feel, what I should do, and how I should be. That belongs to me and to the One who formed me out of the dust of the earth, breathed life into me, and named me good.

The only person I am responsible for and able to change is me.

But in the emotional overload that comes with loss—the amount of change and upheaval that is thrust upon us and the sheer mass of things, people, and feelings there are to deal with—our yearning to return to something that looks and feels normal predisposes us to take on everything.

We want to know it all, do it all, fix it all. We want answers to every question, a resolution for every problem. We want, so much, to put Humpty Dumpty back together again. So we Hoover up all the pieces and, like the seagulls in *Finding Nemo*, claim it all as "Mine!" whether it is in fact ours to own, feel, fix, embrace, and live or not.

We are not in control of every circumstance, nor should we be. It is not all mine to do or fix. Nor is it all yours.

Let go of what you can't control, and set yourself free to engage what you can.

> Each of you must take responsibility for
> doing the creative best you can with your own life.
> Galatians 6:5 MSG

A Prayer for What Is Mine and What Is Not

I have confused it all, Holy One.
Lost my way.
Fallen once again into that old trap of
trying to do it all, fix it all, please them all.

I can't.

All is not mine to do.
I do not have the power, the wherewithal,
the wisdom to fix everything.
If I did somehow manage to make
everyone else happy—but I can't—
I would lose me.

Help me sort it all out.

Give me wisdom to discern what
is mine out of all of this, and the strength to do it.
Give me a clear vision of what is not mine—
what is yours, Author of Life, and what is theirs—
and help me let it go gracefully.

And when I'm tempted to pick it all back up,
remind me again. And again. And again.

Not "Mine!"—not my will, Holy One—but yours.

Part II

TWISTS AND TURNS

*I*n her book *Walking a Sacred Path: Rediscovering the Labyrinth as a Spiritual Practice*, Lauren Artress notes that the labyrinth embedded in the floor of the Chartres Cathedral in France has "thirty-four turns on the path going in to the center. Six of these are semi-right-angle turns, and [the] *twenty-eight others are 180-degree U-turns.*"[8]

Navigating intimate loss is also full of twists and turns. What I *thought* I knew was vastly different from the reality of my experience. Not only did my circumstances change, but my identity changed as well. Things I thought would help didn't always. Even necessary positive changes generated frustration, backlash, and angst. What were innocuous, inconsequential events and circumstances for others turned out to be land mines for me.

---

8 Artress, *Walking a Sacred Path*, 58, emphasis mine.

All of those things necessitated U-turns—rethinking, reorient-ing, turning around. Yet those U-turns did not mean I was lost and on the wrong path. Unlike a maze, there are no dead ends in a lab-yrinth; you can't make a "wrong" turn. As long as you keep putting one foot in front of the other, you will find your way to the center and back out. This proved true for my grief as well. No matter which side of those fine lines I was on, there were lessons to be learned and insights to be gained.

Chapter 5

THERE IS A FINE LINE BETWEEN FAITH AND DOUBT.

Invitation: Befriend unknowing.

The minute my husband told me he thought there might be something wrong, I knew. We had no diagnosis at that point, no idea what "it" was, but I knew, that instant, he was dying.

The vague singular symptom he had—some numbness and tingling in the extremities on his right side—sounded suspiciously like a TIA or stroke, and that's what the Prompt Care physician at our clinic said the next morning when he sent us to the emergency room to get things checked out. I tried to hang on to that explanation as we started the barrage of tests: basic neurological function screenings, blood work, CT scan, and MRI. Ten minutes after the MRI was finished, my worst fears were confirmed when the ER physician came in and said we "needed to find the cancer someplace else" because people "don't just turn up with brain tumors out of the blue," and then she paged the neurosurgeon on call.

They didn't find cancer anywhere else. Just the "lesions on his brain," as the neurosurgeon so quaintly referred to them—one on the brain stem, one in the back of his head, one buried in the center of his brain, and one in the left frontal lobe. Bill declined the brain-stem biopsy the neurosurgeon wanted to perform and left the hospital two days later. We got a referral from our primary care physician for a second opinion and made an appointment at a nationally renowned medical center an hour and a half away.

According to the doctor we saw there, it was impossible to know for sure what we were dealing with without a biopsy. "It could be what they think it is—something metastasized from someplace else," he said, "or it could just be an infection or a fungus. We won't know until we look."

Ever the eternal optimist, my husband interpreted this as a hopeful sign. Maybe it was just a fungus! I wanted, more than anything in the world, to believe things would be all right, but in my heart of hearts—indeed, in the very marrow of my bones—I knew there was nothing they could do and he was never going to get well.

And this—this is where boatloads of guilt got laid on with a trowel. How was it that I could know beyond a shadow of a doubt the minute Bill expressed his initial concern that he was seriously, irretrievably, horribly, fatally ill and not have noticed anything amiss in the weeks and months leading up to that moment?

"Have you not known? Have you not heard?" asked the prophet Isaiah (Isa. 40:28 RSV). In my case, apparently not. I was as clueless as Kit Harington's *Game of Thrones* character, whose companion Ygritte regularly comments on his lack of comprehension with the signature line, "You know nothing, Jon Snow!" Or if you prefer a more generational analogy, there's always Sergeant Schultz's classic response in the 1960s sitcom *Hogan's Heroes*: "I know nothing! I see nothing!"

I did not see or hear *anything* in the previous days, weeks, and months that told me things were not as they should be. I have no idea how I could have missed it. There must have been *something*, but at the time I didn't see it. And I cannot fathom why I could not see it.

My intuition was correct. He did not get well. And the diagnosis and his subsequent decline was even more devastating than my initial worst fears, which were horrible enough. Our lives completely upended, nothing was normal, nothing made sense. Like Blinkin in *Robin Hood: Men in Tights*, I was guessing—about everything. There was no longer anything I could count on, including the one thing I assumed I would always have: my faith.

Bill's out-of-left-field diagnosis left me feeling completely abandoned by God, unable to sense the Sacred's presence in any tangible way and wrestling constantly, Jacob-like, with an endless stream of questions and doubts. I—the pastor!—was too overwhelmed (and too mentally and physically exhausted) to even pray. I could feel the prayers of others but could not utter my own, at least not in the traditional sense of praying. I—the wordsmith!—found myself held mute by the enormity of what was happening to the man I had loved since the moment I'd laid eyes on him at a high school music contest way back in 1971.

Had I crossed that fine line between faith and doubt and now, on the wrong side of it, become some unholy hybrid of Judas the Betrayer and Thomas the Doubter? Was my husband's terminal diagnosis and looming death somehow my fault, this horror visited upon us because of my intuition, which I now labeled as a lack of faith?

I didn't know.

My entire life was one big question mark.

Bill had no questions whatsoever. Trusting God implicitly, he made it clear he was completely at peace with any outcome: divine healing, medical intervention with a positive outcome, or being told this was the end of his life. He never complained. He never expressed regret or said, "I wish I would have . . ." He never railed at God. He never once asked why, though I silently screamed it every hour of every day. From minute one, he kept telling us, "Don't worry about me. I know where I'm going, and I'll be fine."

Even though there was no clinical evidence it would help, the doctors offered treatment, but Bill chose not to pursue it. He insisted, "If I don't know anybody, if I can't talk to anybody, if I can't do anything, I'm done! And I'm okay with that." His every word and act mirrored Job's assertion: "Though he slay me, yet will I trust in him (Job 13:15 KJV).

My spiritual and emotional state resembled a modern-day paraphrase of the quote so often attributed to St. Teresa of Avila: "If this is the way you treat your friends, no wonder you don't have many!"[9]

Being on what I thought was the wrong side of that fine line between faith and doubt was sheer torture. Where I came from, faith was simple and straightforward: You believed. You prayed. God took care of it. If that wasn't what happened, then you either didn't believe enough, didn't pray long enough, didn't pray hard enough, or all of the above. Doubts were as bad as sins; in my case—because I was a pastor—I judged they were even worse.

---

9 An original source for this story can be found in *The Life of St. Teresa*, trans. Alice Lady Lovat (London: Herbert & Daniel, 1912), 548.

As a "faith professional," it was my perception—and, I assumed, the perception of everyone else—that I should know the Divine's mind and have answers for every question, or at least be able to find them. Prayer should flow effortlessly from my heart and lips, trust should be ever-present and unwavering, faith solid and unshakeable. I was never supposed to be afraid, never get mad at or question God. I should have been able to take that terminal diagnosis in stride, with complete calm and trusting serenity—certain, like everyone else, that with all the prayers being lifted on his behalf, Bill would certainly be healed.

That's not where I was. I was filled with doubt and shame, served up daily with a side of fear and liberally garnished with anxiety. I should have known better, I kept telling myself, and I certainly should have *done* better. Should have had my s*&! together and kept my s*&! together. Ever willing to extend grace and mercy to others, I had none for myself.

I told no one about how spectacularly (I thought) I'd failed. Not Bill—the one person I could, and always did, tell everything—because he no longer had the cognitive capacity to understand, and I didn't want to upset him. Not anyone else, because I couldn't face the rejection I was sure would come when they found out what a fraud I was. Certainly not the Holy One, who didn't seem to be listening anyway.

Admitting you don't know when you're one of the ones who is supposed to know sounds and feels like defeat. At the time, I was sure it meant only one thing: I was a loser, the worst pastor—the worst person—on the planet.

Not so.

As I've lived into this loss that is now part of my life, I've learned that what I was feeling was not abnormal, immoral, or bad. As Bill and I heard on the many Marriage Encounter weekends we attended, "Feelings are neither right nor wrong; they just are." I felt how I felt: lost and abandoned, like God was a million miles away. That didn't mean I was errant or incompetent or dysfunctional. Being a pastor who felt those things did not mean I'd traded in my membership as a servant of God. I was simply a human being, being human. There is no shame in that.

Nor is there any shame in calling into question what you believe—*doubting*, as the world labels it. Doubt is not the opposite of faith. Anything that keeps you asking and seeking is, at its heart, an act of faith, a sign that believing still matters.

Owning the fact that you don't have all the answers—and may not even know all the questions—is likewise not a point of failure but a life-giving act of relationship, an invitation to dialogue. The point at which we stop trying to do it, fix it, and figure it all out ourselves is the point where the Holy can begin to work within us.

Looking back now, several years down the road, I can say with assurance that even when it seemed God was absent, the Holy One was there, blessing me and keeping me during those dark days, guiding me through the "valley of the shadow of death," companioning me as I walked the labyrinth of loss, encouraging me, supporting me, holding me up through the prayers of others when I couldn't pray myself.

I would not have made it on my own.

Lord, I believe; help thou mine unbelief.

Mark 9:24 KJV

A Prayer for Not Knowing

What time is it, Holy One?
I do not know.
The hours run together, all awash in tears.

Is it yesterday or tomorrow?
Last week or next?

I do not know, Sacred Presence.
About anything.

I do not know how or why or when or where.

Everything cloudy, nothing certain,
I flounder—minute to minute, day to day—in
this pea soup of the soul,
not sure what to do, how to be.

I cannot find you either.

Beliefs and assurances I thought I could count on
crumble in my hands, leaving nothing to hang on to.
I no longer know what is real, what is true, what is right.

I do not even know, at this moment, if you hear or care,
but not knowing what else to do,
I cry to you.

Gather me up in your everlasting arms.
Shelter me under your wings.
Tend and nurture me until I can see you again,
feel you again, trust you again.

I believe, Lord. Help thou my unbelief.

Chapter 6

THERE IS A FINE LINE BETWEEN CONSCIENTIOUS AND COMPULSIVE.

Invitation: Move beyond your default setting.

Individual and unique, no two of us are alike. As my friend Jen at CobbleWorks says, "We're all unicorns!"

Deeply embedded in that individuality are the coping mechanisms we employ to help us deal with life and all its twists and turns. Mine is organization. I love the promise of order and accomplishment the lines, boxes, and time slots on planner pages and lists evoke. Some think out loud; I think on paper. I have to write it down. Make a list—or several! Chronological. Hierarchical. Topical. Color coded, even!

When Bill's diagnosis and death changed everything in my life overnight, I automatically reverted to that default setting, driven by the mantra, "What do I have to do today?"

Wading through the avalanche of paperwork and tasks that have to be completed when someone dies is, in and of itself, a full-time job. Worried I'd miss something important with the stakes so high—every aspect of my survival on the line—I religiously scripted and planned each day in meticulous detail to be sure I got everything done. When I went back to my pastoral responsibilities a few months later, worship prep, office hours, pastoral care calls, meetings, choir, weddings, and funerals got piled on top of and sandwiched around all the other stuff already in the planner and on the to-do list.

With the best of intentions, without realizing the monster I was creating, I crossed that fine line from conscientious to compulsive without even blinking.

When summer slipped into fall, and the lion's share of the tasks related to Bill's estate were well in hand, the pace slowed down. With more time to think and with the initial numbness that accompanies sudden loss fading, I was brought face-to-face with an onslaught of memories that broke my heart and crushed my spirit a thousand times a day. Waking up and seeing the other side of the bed empty cast a pall on the day before I even put my feet on the floor. Pouring one cup of coffee, not two, reduced me to tears. The vacant love seat where Bill read or watched TV and the unoccupied office chair in front of his computer mocked me every time I walked by them, as did his empty place at the kitchen table.

The silence was deafening.

There were no snippets of hymns playing from his upstairs office as he crafted worship services and worked on the church newsletter. No humming under his breath as he walked from one room to the next. No *1812 Overture* or Dvorak's *New World Symphony* echoing through the kitchen as he updated crop plans, yields, and field histories or surfed the internet. No gaming sound effects as he played *World of Warcraft* with our kids.

It was harvest time by then. Almost every window in our house looked over the fields my husband had farmed for virtually his entire life. He should have been out there driving the combine, and he was not. It became obvious there was no way I could stay by myself—our children lived eleven hundred miles away—in the home we'd shared for nearly forty years. I revisited the discussions Bill and I had that spring about retiring and relocating, and I started making plans to move.

Within the space of four months, I had written my letter of resignation, completed my eighteen-and-a-half-year pastorate, bought a house four states away in Florida, packed, and relocated to the city where our daughter lived.

When the moving van drove away from my new home, I congratulated myself on my ability—thanks to my meticulous planning and my exhaustive and copious lists—to get things done.

Yay me! I can do hard things!

(Yes, like the butler—Tim Curry's character—in the movie *Clue*, "I'm shouting! I'm shouting! I'm shouting!")

I thought I'd made it—that it was all downhill from there. I mistakenly equated having handled those big-ticket things with having dealt, once and for all, with my grief and loss.

I hadn't done that at all.

I always regarded my organizational bent as a gift or a skill; my husband thought of it more along the lines of a personality flaw or a vice.

He was closer to right than I ever wanted to admit.

With nothing to fill the hours now, all those things I hadn't had time to process or allowed myself to feel, all those things I thought I'd handled but had only shoved aside—plus a host of other things I never fully understood about myself—came bubbling to the surface.

I was finally able to see that what I had called my schedule functioned, in reality, like a straitjacket. Bound by those planned-to-the-minute blocks of time that filled my calendar and the endless task lists I so carefully crafted each day, there was no wiggle room.

As I sat with that realization, the blank pages of my planner mocking me from their spot on the desk next to the phone, I discovered that behind my organizational bent were feelings of powerlessness, anxiety, and fear. Even before, but especially after, Bill's diagnosis and death, I'd used the calendar and the clock to (try to) control my circumstances, to filter and meter my emotions.

It was a colossal failure.

My compulsive organizational efforts did not—could not—keep life from happening. Regardless of my plans and my rigid execution of them, my husband still got sick, still died. There was nothing I could do about that; no amount of planning or list making had the power to change that reality or bring him back.

It also became clear that just because my calendar was full and I was occupied from dawn until dark, that did not mean I was doing what was truly necessary. If something was on the list or given a time slot, I made sure it got done—or at least tried to—*no matter what.* As a result, each day was so overbooked with so many things I thought I had to do, there was no time for me to think, feel, or just *be.*

And buried under all my plans and lists, my grief was still there, waiting for me to slow down long enough to notice it. I had to put down—set aside—my rabid scheduling habit and codependence with my to-do lists.

I now consider myself a recovering planner. I still have planners—yes, more than one—and I still make lists. Appointments get written down so I don't forget them and I don't overbook myself. But instead of trying to script and control my life by plotting every second of every day, much of what winds up on those pages gets filled in after the fact, a record of what I spent my time on, not the dictatorial enumeration of how much I had to do to feel like a worthwhile human being.

Because the other thing that came out of this was the realization that I also used my to-do list as a gauge of my self-worth. If I got to the end of the day and everything was done, things were fine. If tasks had not been marked off, I berated myself, employing the language of failure with a broad brush. I couldn't simply say I'd failed to complete something on the list; in my perception, those undone tasks meant *I* was a failure.

I'm learning to be gentle with myself, to offer—and accept!—grace. My perception of failure and what it means has changed as well. Failure is not the overwhelming negative I thought it was; it is not evidence of incompetence, nor is it any commentary on my worth as a human being. Rather, it is an opportunity to learn, an invitation to try again. If there are things I don't get done by the end of the day, it is not the end of the world. I have seen what was, for me, the end of the world, and that is *not* it.

The truth is, there are only twenty-four hours in a day, and we finite human creatures have limits of mental, physical, and emotional energy we cannot push ourselves beyond. We are not Instant Pots, nor can we run nonstop at "ludicrous speed," as Mel Brooks called it in his *Star Wars* spoof, *Spaceballs*. While it's helpful to have some sort of guide and rhythm in life that helps us tend to what is necessary to keep life and limb together, plans and lists cannot control our circumstances and keep our emotions in check, nor are they intended to.

Your worth as a person is not defined by what you did or did not get crossed off your to-do list on any given day. If you got everything on the list handled, yay, you! If you couldn't get dressed, pick up the phone, or look at the mail—if all you did was ugly cry all day—so be it.

You can try again tomorrow.

> [God's] mercies never come to an end;
> they are new every morning.
> Lamentations 3:22–23 RSV

A Prayer for Time

Deliver me, Holy One, from my
overinvestment in the calendar and clock.
Save me from ordering my days exclusively by
the tick of the second hand and the
lines on the planner page.

Turn my focus from the tyranny of the "important"—
temptations and distractions garbed in seemingly urgent clothing—
to what is truly necessary for my life, health, and well-being.

Open my eyes to both chronos and kairos,
that I may live "in due time,"
by the rhythms of your creative Spirit,
where days are both now and forever—
which means there is never a time when I am outside your care.

Remind me that your love is unconditional
and without end, my worth not dependent on
what I do or don't.

And when I slip back into plotting and scurrying,
slow me down; refocus my attention.
Walk with me as I start over again,
your grace and mercy fresh
on my mind and filling my heart.

Chapter 7

THERE IS A FINE LINE BETWEEN COMPLIMENT AND CRITICISM.

Invitation: Honor the embodied.

*I*n the months following my husband's death, I lost fifty-plus pounds. It wasn't something I intentionally set out to do; it was just one more thing that happened because my entire life changed literally in an instant.

For Bill and me, sharing conversation over a meal was one of the highlights of our life together. It was holy ground and sacred space. Because of the way our schedules were configured, Thursday nights had become our date night. We'd unwind over a leisurely dinner, talking about everything and nothing before the weekend flurry of church activities and Sunday worship. It was an exquisite treat to share good food, fine wine, and deep conversation with the love of my life, and I enjoyed it to the hilt.

Without him and those conversations that sustained me as much as the food I consumed, I dreaded mealtimes. The kitchen table, where we'd communed daily, became a black hole that sucked the life out of me every time I sat down.

Eating out without him was emotionally exhausting and a logistical nightmare. We lived "in the middle of nowhere," as Ree Drummond says in her intro to *The Pioneer Woman* cooking show on the Food Network. There weren't many dining options in the small town closest to our home; our favorite restaurant was nearly an hour's drive away.

Cooking for myself was no better. Trying to figure out what I wanted to eat, when eating alone was so painful and lonely, was an exercise in frustration. What sounded good in the store didn't when I got home, or by then I was too tired to fix it.

It was far easier to just throw some salad on a plate and call it lunch or dinner. So that's what I did, and that's when the pounds started melting away.

I absolutely needed to lose that weight. My health improved dramatically as a result.

Yet that necessary and positive change was fraught with anxiety and pain.

Most people, when they run into someone they know—particularly after a significant life event—say something like "Good to see you!" or "How are you?" Instead, absent of any sort of greeting, people would walk up to me and blurt, "How much weight have you lost? Are you eating?"

Sigh. Nice to see you too.

The comment that (almost always) followed was just as disturbing: "Well, you look good!"

I know those words were motivated by genuine concern, intended to make me feel better.

They didn't.

Instead, they added worry and angst to my already painful existence. If I now looked *so good* that people felt compelled to comment on it, how bad must I have looked before?

Like the proverbial two-edged sword, the comments cut deeply, exposing not only the misfit, fish-out-of-water feelings the radical change in my circumstances had created, but also laying bare body and self-image issues I didn't even know I had. Already unsure of my identity, ability, and place in the world after Bill's death, the remarks raised questions about my mental and physical health, caused me to second-guess every clothing purchase, and made me agonize daily over what to wear and whether I looked okay or not.

Bill was always able to reorient my thinking from *what wasn't* and *why* to *what was* and *what could be,* always able to show me the good. Without him there to reassure me, those external voices and the Organizational Perfectionist in my head took over, and the message was clear: Before, I was too heavy; now I was too thin. No matter how I was, it wasn't good enough.

My body became an additional source of pain. I tried to ignore it, to disassociate myself from the comments and their implications, the worry about what I looked like or didn't, and what others thought of me. I wanted it all to just go away.

It wouldn't.

What I didn't understand at the time—what I've learned since— is that grief is not singular and one-dimensional. It is not just emotional but is an embodied process as well.

All-inclusive and all-encompassing, the effects and fallout of loss worm their way into every detail of life. Insinuating themselves into every circumstance and conversation, they affect you mentally, emotionally, spiritually, and physically. The rapid weight loss I experienced was just one thing on a long list of physiological expressions of grief I experienced.

At various moments—when I heard the words *brain tumors*, when I watched the love of my life take that last breath, when I saw his body in the casket and his name on the grave marker—I had the sensation of being slammed in the chest by a boulder or crashing into a brick wall at a hundred miles an hour, leaving my heart sinking, my stomach churning, my head spinning.

Exhaustion dogged my steps regardless of how many hours of sleep I got or didn't. For some, grief is marked by extended periods of insomnia. I was able to go to bed, fall asleep, and sleep all night nearly every night, yet I awoke each morning feeling like I hadn't rested at all.

There were times when I literally couldn't breathe, when it felt as though an elephant was sitting on my chest and my lungs couldn't expand far enough to take in air.

Being surprised by waves of intense emotion left my heart pounding and my pulse racing.

I felt mentally foggy—airheaded and spacey, unable to concentrate for more than a few minutes at a time.

Bodily functions sometimes didn't. Or they functioned too much, too often.

Splitting headaches were a regular occurrence, especially on days filled with paperwork or decision-making.

I experienced a pronounced lack of energy and physical stamina.

Even though I'd lost a significant number of pounds, I felt heavy, weighed down, as if the weight of the entire world was on my shoulders.

Random aches and pains showed up for no apparent reason, leaving me feeling battered and bruised, as if I'd been run over by a truck.

The combination of raw grief plus the painful comments about my appearance was a devastating double whammy. When you're in that much pain, the temptation to retreat, to disengage, to hole up and lick your wounds is strong.

Don't.

The body has as much to say about grief as your thoughts, your emotions, your spirit, and your heart do. Wondrous and miraculous, it can alert us to problems, even heal itself. Commanding our attention more readily than other things, the body can help us find our way through the labyrinth of loss, reminding us to slow down and not rush through our grief, to take our time and pay attention to what is happening to us—to all of the parts of us.

Listen to your body. Pay attention to it. Learn from it. Make peace with it. Accept it. Honor it.

> May the God of peace himself sanctify you entirely;
> and may your spirit and soul and body be kept
> sound and blameless.
>
> 1 Thessalonians 5:23 NRSV

A Prayer for the Body

Stop the world, Holy One. I want to get off.
No longer comfortable in my own skin, I want it all to go away:
the isolation; the misfit, never-good-enough feelings;
the cutting comments that slice to the core.

The anguish, the groaning, the weeping, the distress.
The weak eyes and failing strength,
the crumbling bones and sinking heart.
I'm broken and spilled out, dry and weary.

Crushed and exhausted, I feel it all. All the time.

But you have too, Sacred Presence.
You chose an embodied existence,
lived, experienced, embraced it all.
You are, after all, Alpha and Omega—beginning and end,
before and beyond and everything in between.

You hungered and thirsted, ate and drank.
You celebrated weddings, welcomed children, wept at Lazarus's tomb.
You felt anger and compassion, joy and sorrow, hope and despair.
You were pierced, heart and soul as well as body.

And through it all, you remained true
to your calling as child of God.

I can do no less.

Help me embrace this flesh—
fearfully and wonderfully made in your image.
Strengthen me, Holy One, spirit, soul, and body,
that I may walk with you in newness of life,
no matter my circumstances or appearance.

Chapter 8

THERE IS A FINE LINE BETWEEN HAVING EVERYTHING YOU NEED AND HAVING TOO MUCH STUFF.

Invitation: Trust your worth.

My experience with the first furniture store I chose to do business with when I made my move south, which shall remain nameless, was less than stellar. Considerably. When it takes longer to get a dresser and two nightstands from a major manufacturer than it does a special order of couches and chairs, there is an issue. I understand waiting six to eight weeks for custom-upholstered furniture pieces to arrive. I do not understand waiting that long—and then some—for furniture that is mass produced and supposedly in stock, as in *sitting in the warehouse as we speak.*

For the most part, while it was extremely annoying, it was not an insurmountable problem. I had plenty of hangers and a spacious walk-in closet. It seemed a bit precious to have jeans, sweatpants, and nightgowns hanging beside dresses, skirts, suit jackets, and dress slacks, but it kept things neat and orderly, which is one of the things I live for, so that part didn't bother me. What grated on my nerves—*and still does when I think about it*—was having to keep my underwear and jewelry in boxes on the closet floor. Not having a place for your most intimate and personal possessions can be completely unnerving, especially for someone like me, who thrives on order.

My grief made it a million times worse. When you're grieving, it is often a huge challenge just to make the decision to get out of bed and get dressed. Being forced to rummage through a box on the closet floor to find underwear magnified those feelings of being rudderless, alone, and lost in the wilderness to a horrifying degree.

I called the customer service number repeatedly but got nowhere. The nameless, shameless furniture store couldn't have cared less. They weren't the ones rummaging through a box on the closet floor every morning in order to be appropriately dressed, and my discomfort at having to do so was of no concern to them. Six and a half long weeks later, the dresser and nightstands finally arrived, and I was able to get everything off the floor and put away where it belonged. But it will be much longer than six and a half weeks before I forget what that felt like.

A recurring theme in the Psalms is the writer's plea, "How long, O Lord?" I ask that question too, but more often my refrain on my trek through the labyrinth of loss has been "How much, O Lord?" I've asked it a million different times in a million different ways about a million different things as I've trod every incarnation of that fine line between having too much and not enough.

In the beginning, after my husband's diagnosis but before his death, it was "How much of this misery, this decline, this living hell on earth can he take? And how much can I?"

Within hours of him taking his last breath—and for months afterward—I wondered, "How much *can* one person cry? Is there an upper limit on tears?"

The "How much?" questions continued as I packed to move. Before he died, we'd already begun seriously discussing what retirement would look like for us and how soon we could start spending winters somewhere warm and where at least one of our children lived. After we returned from our family reunion at Disney World, Bill spent hours on end looking at houses in Florida. One gray, late February day, he called me out of my upstairs office and walked me through each room of our home, pointing to all the major pieces of furniture and asking whether we were taking them with us when we moved or leaving them behind.

That memory holds the biggest "How much?" question of all— the one that still haunts me to this day. How much did Bill know about how sick he was? Did he know? Was he trying to get the move completed before he became incapacitated so I wouldn't have to do it by myself?

I have no idea.

We'd discussed the big things—the piano, appliances, furniture—but I still had all the little things to deal with. I once again went from room to room, asking myself, "How much of this lifetime of stuff do I take with me?" I was constantly yanked backward down memory lane, even as I was trying to move forward into what was left of the rest of my life.

To get through it, I played my own version of Twenty Questions applied with a Marie Kondo mindset. Do I love it? Do I like it? (Do I even know what it is?) Do I need it? (How many casserole dishes does one need, anyway? I honestly have no idea.) Do I use it? Do I use it often enough to justify paying someone to drag it eleven hundred miles? Is it still functional, or is it "past it"? Is it possible to let this go, or does it hold too many memories? Will my kids or grandkids want this someday? If it comes with me, will there be a place to put it? If it stays behind, what do I do with it now? Donate? (But does anybody really want this thing?) Pitch? (But it seems too good to throw away!)

I had been there and done that. Asked and answered all the questions, reasoned through the dilemmas, made the hard decisions, figured it all out. I was livid that the furniture company's blatant misrepresentation of when I could expect my furniture to arrive and lack of concern when it didn't had me walking that fine line, wrestling with those "How much?" questions all over again.

Under any other circumstance, being without furniture and having things in boxes on the closet floor wouldn't have been that big a deal. Had he been there, my husband would have turned it into a joke about camping out in the house. I hate camping with a purple passion—"I camp at the Westin" is my mantra—*and he knew that*. But he would have said something anyway. In fact, he would have taken great delight in bringing it up, those blue eyes dancing as he said it, and would have made me laugh about it too.

That was the real problem.

He wasn't there to make the joke.

It wasn't about how much stuff I had or didn't or the particular pieces of furniture themselves. It was about the fact that without him there to share the experience, nothing mattered as much. Every time I walked into the bedroom (which had no furniture in it except the bed, which I now slept in alone), every time I opened the closet door and saw those boxes on the floor, every time I needed to dress or change clothes, what was eating me alive far beyond the inconvenience was the constant reminder of Bill's absence and how meaningless life—and I—felt without him.

Grief isolates in a manner few other things do, leaving those in its midst feeling not just lonely and not just alone but completely inconsequential. Like Frank Cross, Bill Murray's character in the movie *Scrooged*, our experience and emotional state is so "other" from the rest of the world's, "nobody gets [us]." When it happens over and over again, every day and in any and every circumstance, you don't just *feel* alone and of no value; you begin to believe that's the truth about who you are.

That's what those six long weeks without a dresser and nightstands internalized in me. My empty bedroom and those boxes on the closet floor were visible symbols of just how much I didn't matter, proof no one cared.

When the furniture finally arrived, I was able to finish decorating the room, to arrange all those trinkets and treasures that make a house a home. As I was hanging the last picture—the print of Van Gogh's *Still Life with Bible* I'd gifted Bill one Father's Day, his favorite, the one he spent a full thirty minutes pondering when we toured the Van Gogh Museum in Amsterdam—something clicked. In it, Van Gogh's father's Bible lies open on a table, a copy of Émile Zola's *La Joie de vivre* next to it. That painting—which I can see from any place in the room and walk by multiple times a day—caused me to think of Bill every time I saw it, a tangible and powerful reminder of how much I mattered, not just to him, but also to the Holy One.

We humans are finite creatures. We think in finite terms. We parse, we measure, we quantify, asking those "How much? How many? How long?" questions all the time. About everything. And the view is often narrow, the numbers small. In Matthew 18:21–35, Peter quizzed Jesus about how many times he was required to forgive. "Seven, maybe?" he wondered. "Seventy-seven," Jesus said, but the footnote to that verse in my study Bible reads, "Or seventy *times* seven." Peter thought in small, finite terms—what he could count on two hands. Christ multiplied exponentially.

In fact, the entire biblical narrative is one long litany of the lavish and abundant love of our Creator, from the very beginning, when we are formed out of the dust of the earth and named good, to the very end, where we are again, yet, still, always, named as God's own people.

The grace and mercy of the Lord is free, unlimited, and available to all. Always. We are all worth it, *and then some.*

Our circumstances—and how we interpret them—can lead us to think, as *Saturday Night Live's* Wayne and Garth did, that "we're not worthy!" and no one cares. Don't believe it. Regardless of your circumstances or possessions (or the lack thereof), regardless of what customer service tells you or doesn't, you and how you feel matter.

You are worth more than many sparrows.

Matthew 10:31 NIV

A Prayer for Us Sparrows

I feel lost in the shuffle, Holy One.
Inconsequential.
As anonymous as a singular star
in the vast universe,
one lonely grain of sand on the seashore.

Yet you do notice. You are cognizant of each one.

You, whose eye is ever on even the lowly sparrow,
remind me again, anew, each day,
that I matter.
That you watch over me as well.

That regardless of what others say or what I tell myself,
like the rest of your children scattered
around the world, I too am precious in your sight.

That even though I walk the valley of the shadow,
tread the labyrinth of loss,
face pestilence and plague, night terrors and day arrows,
you will companion me, be present with me.

Remind me daily—minute by minute—
that your steadfast love and mercies never cease,
that you will never leave or forsake me,
that because you love me, I matter.

Part III

MOVING THE CHAIRS

The famed labyrinth in the Cathedral of Our Lady of Chartres in Chartres, France, is massive, yet it can still be difficult to find. Much of the time, it is covered with chairs—as many as 256 of them.[10] In order to find the path and walk the labyrinth, you have to move the chairs.

The process of finding your way forward after losing someone you love—walking the labyrinth of grief and loss—also requires us to move the chairs. Loss is universal. Everybody dies and everybody loses people they care about. But grief and loss are experienced in highly personal ways, and every situation is different. What was helpful and comforting for me and my family may be anathema for you and yours. What worked in one circumstance won't in another.

---

10 Artress, *Walking a Sacred Path*, 4–5.

We have to discover our own path—make our own way—in our own way and at our own pace.

And that path can be as challenging to discern and navigate as moving hundreds of chairs off the cathedral floor. The immediate and radical change in circumstances that follows a loved one's death begets change in every facet of life, both what you do and how you do it. What was once familiar and straightforward is now fraught with uncertainty and confusion. Treated by culture as a singular occurrence—something you "get over"—for those living it, in reality, grief is long-term and both exponential and cumulative. There are no timetables or formulas for grieving, nor is there a standard route that will take you from where you are straight into the rest of your life.

Chapter 9

THERE IS A FINE LINE BETWEEN SOLITUDE AND HEARTBREAKING, SOUL-CRUSHING LONELINESS.

Invitation: Come home to you.

For a long time, I couldn't see that fine line between solitude and loneliness.

I saw *them*. I saw them everywhere I went, and I hated them. I hated them all. Whether it was the Murphy's Law effect—anything that can go wrong, will—or just bad timing, I, the painfully, unhappily single, found myself surrounded by couples in the days and months following Bill's death. From the fourteen-year-olds draped all over each other at the mall to the octogenarians toddling, hands clasped, through Target and Sam's, I couldn't "swing a dead cat," as my grandmother would say, without hitting a twosome.

In all honesty, *hate* is not the right word. I didn't know any of them well enough to truly hate them. They were total strangers, not even in the category of casual acquaintances, yet the vision of them walking in sync, exchanging knowing looks, laughing at inside jokes to which only they knew the punch lines brought me great pain.

Each day between my husband's unexpected diagnosis and his death less than three months later brought its own level of horror as he disappeared before my eyes, minute by minute. Not only did he drive us to the hospital for the biopsy—an hour and a half away—he also made two trips to the airport to pick up our kids later that afternoon in St. Louis traffic. When we left four days later, he was unable to walk without assistance. (There were, in fact, serious questions in the first forty-eight hours after surgery as to whether he'd be able to come home at all or if he would need to be placed in a skilled nursing facility.) Within two and a half weeks of our return home, he was in a wheelchair; twelve days later, they delivered the hospital bed; less than three weeks after that, he was completely bedridden, the articulate, funny, gifted extemporaneous speaker with a one-liner for everything no longer able to put three words together in a way that made sense.

It was all *beyond* horrible, but the hardest part was not those days spent walking through the valley of the shadow of his approaching death. The hardest part was afterwards, when I was left utterly and completely alone. His illness lasted just a handful of days: from March 14, when he told me something *might* be wrong, to that moment just before 4:00 p.m. on June 12, when he took his last breath. His passing itself was a mere moment—breathing, and then not, just like that. But the aloneness that was now my reality dragged on and on and on, without end. Everywhere I looked, everything I did, everything I touched—every decision, every task, every circumstance—brought yet another reminder that he was gone *and he was never coming back.*

And without him, I no longer had any idea who I was.

We married so young, I barely remember life before becoming his wife.

We married so young, we literally grew up together, my psyche forever altered and imprinted by the infusing of our lives.

We married so young, but we also married the person who was our best friend, and losing my husband *and* my confidant, my rock, my main source of support, the one who loved me unconditionally and always had my back, set me adrift in ways I never imagined possible. I had no idea where to turn when the one I would have turned to in the wake of trauma of that depth was the one who was now gone forever.

Gilda Radner says, "It's always something," in her memoir of the same title. She is right. But in grieving intimate loss, within each of those "somethings" are fine lines, layers, wheels within wheels. It isn't just one thing. It's one thing after another after another, all interconnected and intertwined.

I didn't just lose my spouse; I lost my best friend, my social system, my identity.

I went from knowing exactly who I was to a *Twilight Zone* existence, the oh-so-familiar tasks that had defined my days morphing into an endless litany of Things I've Never Done Before, Things I've Never Done by Myself Before, Things I Don't Know How to Do, Things I Didn't Even Know I Needed to Do, and Things Too Horrible for Words. (If I see a spider now, I have to murder it myself!)

With every detail of my life and every moment of my day-to-day existence different than it had ever been, I no longer fit in any of the places I used to. A stranger in the new country of widowhood, I had no idea who I was or how to be.

No one else knew either. Not sure what to say or do, afraid of upsetting me (read: saying or doing something that caused me to cry), worried they were bothering me, beset by survivor guilt, and without a common denominator—Bill—to keep us together, connections gradually disappeared.

One glance at all those people with their spouses, partners, companions, soulmates, confidants, significant others, and BFFs accentuated and exaggerated my aloneness. For me, there was no fine line between them; solitude *equaled* heartbreaking, soul-crushing loneliness, absence, separation, isolation.

But my perception of what solitude is and does was inaccurate. There is more to solitude than being apart or alone, and it is not all negative. It has as much to do with who we are as it does how and where we are. Parker Palmer says, "Solitude does not necessarily mean living apart from others; rather, it means never living apart from one's self. It is not about the absence of other people—it is about being *fully present to ourselves*, whether or not we are with others."[11]

---

11 Parker Palmer, *A Hidden Wholeness: The Journey Toward an Undivided Life* (San Francisco: Jossey-Bass, 2008), 55, emphasis mine.

Scottish philosopher Alasdair MacIntyre puts it this way: "I can only answer the question 'What am I to do?' if I can answer the prior question 'Of what story or stories do I find myself a part?'"[12]

Who am I now, and what is my story to live and tell?

While they were descriptive, the roles and titles I previously relied on for my sense of identity neither were nor are the be-all, end-all of my existence. There is more to who I am than a declaration of occupation, a list of degrees, or a fistful of pictures of my children and grandchildren. Who I am is more than my personality traits, a diagnosis, my hobbies and interests, the external events that have been visited upon me, or any of the labels, slots, and cubbyholes culture uses to categorize.

Mirroring the physical traversing of a labyrinth from the entrance to the center and back out again, in order to find my way back home to myself, I had to find my center—to search out the real me—and discern what was my story to tell, what was mine alone to offer the world.

We human creatures are both breath of heaven and dust of the earth, a cumulative expression of the generations who have gone before us, further shaped and impacted by our own lived experiences. In order to understand what makes us *us*, we have to mine the depths of all of those experiences. We have to look at the whole story of our lives.

---

12 Alasdair MacIntyre, *After Virtue*, 3rd ed. (Notre Dame, IN: University of Notre Dame Press, 2007), 216.

I didn't know all of mine. Some parts were fuzzy; others were blank. Both my parents had been married previously. They'd lived half their lives before marrying and having me, and I knew nothing about their lives in those earlier years or how that history impacted our family. So I went "back to the beginning," as Vizzini says in Rob Reiner's fairy-tale movie *The Princess Bride*, and started digging.

I found explanations and clarity.

I got a healthy dose of perspective.

I was also gifted with solidarity and hope.

My maternal great-great-grandmother was a single mom in 1840s England, which was daunting enough in itself. Then she married my great-great-grandfather in 1850 and gave birth to six more children, two of whom died in infancy. Workers in the Lancashire textile mills, their jobs disappeared when the embargo of America's southern ports stopped cotton shipments during the Civil War. So in April of 1865, they traveled to Liverpool, boarded the *Chancellor*, and set sail for America. She endured a monthlong ocean voyage with more than 575 other people, wrangling children ranging in age from two to fourteen and being in the first trimester of yet another pregnancy, then disembarked in a country where she knew no one and made her way from New York to Chicago, where she rebuilt her life and that of her family.

If she could endure that, I could have professional movers haul my stuff to the new home waiting for me four states away, where my daughter lived, and survive too.

"But wait!" as direct-marketing and infomercial guru Ron Popeil of Veg-O-Matic and Pocket Fisherman fame said, "There's more!" In her story, pieced together from church records and entries in my grandmother's Bible, I discovered a legacy of faith running through my family line that is longer, deeper, and wider than I ever realized. It was a glimpse of resurrection. To find tangible evidence that faith was an integral part of the lives of those from whom I come helped redeem and restore mine.

In *Labyrinths from the Outside In*, Donna Schaper says, "The power to heal is the power of focus. It is to live from the place that really matters."[13]

That place is the center, and that's where grief takes us, if we will let it. Finding and coming home to myself, the "real" me, is a lifelong process. But in learning the stories of those who have gone before me, I've been given valuable clues and insights about who and Whose I am. Whatever else I am or may become, my heritage, my identity, and my truth is rooted in this: I belong to the Holy One. I am a child of God.

There are times when what we don't know is as important as the things we do know. In searching out those truths, filling in those gaps, a more complete picture emerges, enabling us to further live into our true identity—to come home to ourselves.

A father to the fatherless, a defender of widows,
is God in his holy dwelling.
God sets the lonely in families [the desolate in a homeland],
he leads out the prisoners with singing.
Psalm 68:5–6 NIV

13 Donna Schaper and Carole Ann Camp, *Labyrinths from the Outside In: Walking to Spiritual Insight* (Woodstock, VT: SkyLight Paths Publishing, 2013), 26.

Who Am I Now?

Without that one person to fill my days,
the one who mattered most to me,
silence defines my experience.

Large, gaping chasms everywhere,
a hole in my heart, blanks in my days.
Absence, not presence.

What defined me before no longer applies.
No one's wife, lover, confidant, muse.
No one's pastor, collaborator, counselor, teacher.

Who am I now?

Questions spill out like ointment
pouring from an alabaster jar.

In this breaking, is there healing?
In this pouring, is there love?
In the silence, yet communion?
In the absence, still a bond?

Yes.
In my heart, at my core, I'm still me.

Singular, but not isolated and alone.
In solitude, to myself much of the time,
yet I am not cut off from the world or life and living.

I no longer have that one person.
But I have people.

I have ancestors and descendants,
family and friends, colleagues and contemporaries,
whose lives are bound to mine by
genetics, relationship, faith,
experience, circumstances, and love.

They know, they affirm, they reflect,
they bring out, they enhance
the essence of me.

I have people.

I have a Trinity of companionship,
always with me and capable of filling every void.
Creator, Christ, Spirit.
Parent, Friend, Comforter.

Tune me ever to your presence, Holy One.
Remind me that even in solitude and silence,
you abide, you commune, you accompany,
that it is in you that I live, move, have my being.

Even you drew away from the crowds, Jesus—
alone, yet still in union with your Creator.
Solitary, I am still me,
and I belong to you.
I no longer have that one person.
But I have people.

I have myself.

Chapter 10

THERE IS A FINE LINE BETWEEN A FEW BUMPS AND BRUISES AND A STAB IN THE HEART.

Invitation: Speak with care.

Death is something all of us go through; even Jesus experienced it. Yet despite its universality, we human creatures have a notoriously difficult time dealing with it—if, in fact, we deal with it at all. (Many don't.) Unless we are funeral directors or chaplains or work in the field of palliative or hospice care, we don't speak about death, dying, loss, and grief on a daily basis. If they are discussed at all, the conversation often resembles a latter-day rehash of Monty Python's "Dead Parrot" sketch, filled with platitudes and clichés that not only don't help, they cause even more grief.

Any other time, I could have taken the platitudes and clichés in stride as well-meaning but unthinking or just differences in theology, the emotional equivalent of a slight bump or bruise. In the midst of raw grief, they trespassed far beyond the fine line that separates minor injury from deep pain, and each one I heard felt like a stab in the heart.

I wish I hadn't been told, "He's in a better place." While I believe that to be true in my husband's case, hearing it only reminded me of the excruciatingly painful fact that he was no longer physically present with me in this place and wouldn't ever be again. That was the last thing I needed at that point in time; every facet of my existence screamed his absence every minute of every day.

I wish I hadn't been told, "Everything happens for a reason," that this was somehow "God's will" or "all part of God's plan." Rather than the loving, compassionate presence Scripture assures us God is, those words made God seem like a capricious bully who purposefully planned and willfully chose to afflict my husband with an aggressive and incurable disease that turned him into an unresponsive vegetable and took his life mere weeks after diagnosis. I can't believe in that God. What I *can* believe, now, is that however Bill's life unfolded and whatever he experienced, God planned to be—and was—present with him in all of it.

I wish I hadn't been told I would understand "someday." As Frederick Buechner says in his book *Wishful Thinking: A Seeker's ABC*, understanding why isn't as helpful as we like to think it is:

> Suppose that God did explain. Suppose that God were to say to Job that the reason the cattle were stolen, the crops ruined, and the children killed was thus and so, spelling everything out right down to and including the case of boils. Job would have his explanation.

And then what?

Understanding in terms of the divine economy why his children had to die, Job would still have to face their empty chairs at breakfast every morning. Carrying in his pocket straight from the horse's mouth a complete theological justification of his boils, he would still have to scratch and burn.[14]

Equally problematic was being assured we'd be together again "someday." It's a lovely sentiment, one I also believe is true, but "someday" was a construct I could not wrap my head around in those early days of raw grief. I couldn't see that far ahead. Hearing it over and over but not being able to envision it only angered and frustrated me; it did nothing to help me get through the current day, which was what I needed most right then (and at times still do).

I wish I hadn't been told, "I know exactly how you feel!" While others may have been in similar circumstances, they didn't know exactly how I felt. No one knew that but me—and there were times even I didn't know *exactly* how I felt. Because of the circumstances of Bill's death, what I did feel (in flashes, between the numbness and shock) was a crazy cocktail of relief, rage, terror, gratitude, guilt, love, joy, uncertainty, peace, resentment, and loneliness overlaid with layer after layer of overwhelming sadness.

I wish I hadn't been given so much advice. Every time I heard tales that started, "And when ____ died, we did ____," and knew I'd done things differently, I began second-guessing my choices, worrying I'd done it all wrong. That just piled another helping of guilt and

14 Frederick Buechner, *Wishful Thinking: A Seeker's ABC*, rev. ed. (San Francisco: HarperOne, 1993), 56–57.

an additional veneer of questions on top of the mountain of sorrow and confusion I was already being crushed under.

The other thing those stories did was turn the tables, making the conversation about the other person and their grief. At times that left me feeling (even more) invisible and inconsequential. On other occasions, due to the intensity of the narrative, I felt obligated to put on my pastor hat, move into pastoral care mode, and take care of them.

It wasn't that the information or experience the other person shared wasn't meaningful and valid. It was. But I did not possess the emotional energy to deal with it. I was not capable, right then, of being the caretaker of someone else's feelings and grief experience. I could barely manage my own.

I wish I hadn't been told I needed to find "closure." I understand the sentiment; people wanted me to be able to move on from where I was. But, again, the language caused additional pain. The way it is used in our culture, *closure* denotes "getting over it," implying a level of finality I find highly distasteful and inaccurate. You don't "get over" loss. You come to terms with it. It becomes part of your life.

The truth is, I don't want to "get over" Bill, forget about him, or lose track of him or anything about him. I never wanted the life I shared with him to come to an end. I haven't stopped loving him, nor do I plan to.

If that's what closure means, then I echo Ebenezer Scrooge's comment to Jacob Marley when his late business partner offered the visiting spirits as a means for Ebenezer's redemption: "I think I'd rather not."

There is no one "right" thing to say, no magic words for speaking about death, dying, grief, and their aftermath. There is nothing anyone can say that will fix this or take away the pain. And despite the universality of death, dying, and bereavement, it is one of the most individualized experiences of our human existence. Like every walk through the labyrinth, each person's grief is unique; one size does not fit all.

What I needed was not words so much as acknowledgment and permission to be who I was, where I was, and to feel what I was feeling. Rather than feeling sorry *for* me, I yearned for people to be present *with* me in all the ugly, messy, raw pain.

If you have to say something (but I promise, you really don't), say you're sorry. I'm sorry this happened too; those words speak to where I am and resonate with my experience. Share a special memory or something you loved about the one that I love. Tell me how much he meant to you; that will mean something to me.

Just be there. That will communicate your care and concern louder and better than any words ever could. Show up; be there, and be present. Listen if I need to talk or scream or wail or rant. Sit with me while I sob. If "sitting with" is not your gift, offer to mow my grass, clean my house, do my laundry, bring dinner, make coffee, do the dishes, or help handle phone calls and visitors. Bring note cards and stamps. House-sit while I'm at the visitation and/or funeral. Take me out for lunch. Do your best to give me honest answers if I ask questions. If you don't know the answer, say so; don't just tell me what you think I need or want to hear.

Later on, when the dust settles, don't assume I'm "fine" or ignore me because you don't know what to say. Don't refrain from asking how I am, but be mindful of how you do so. Counselors and therapists adore open-ended questions because they usually provide more information and context than closed questions, but there are times when open-ended questions are not the best choice, and bereavement has been one of those for me. Being asked "How are you?" is overwhelming. One minute I'm completely fine. The next minute I'm so completely not fine, it defies articulation. There's no way for me to answer that question in the time frame of regular conversation in a way that honestly captures my reality.

In her book *Option B: Facing Adversity, Building Resilience, and Finding Joy*, Sheryl Sandberg suggests asking, "How are you doing *today?*" I agree with her premise, but I would take it even further. My experience in trying to navigate the rapidly shifting sands that make up the landscape of grief has taught me that even just one day may be more real estate than I can wrap my head around. Instead, ask me how I'm doing *at the moment*. Moments feel much more manageable than the unlimited forever implied in that open-ended "How are you doing?" question. If things are not good, I can own that while hanging on to the hope that they may be better later. If things are okay at the moment, I can celebrate that while acknowledging the reality that grief is a lifelong process with ups and downs, ebbs and flows, twists and turns. The Michelob people were right: "Some days are better than others."

Death, dying, and grief are hard to talk about, no matter which side of the conversation you're on. In most cases—I know in mine—the comments weren't meant to be hurtful, nor were those uttering the words uncaring and unfeeling. The very fact that some people were willing to engage when the subject was so painful and difficult was an indication they cared and were seeking to offer a meaningful explanation for what happened and some measure of comfort.

You may hear some of the same things I heard. You may hear worse. What you need to understand is this: Since our culture doesn't talk openly about death, dying, and loss, most people don't know how. The people who do—we mourners who are constantly walking that fine line and are painfully aware of what is helpful and what is not—don't always have the physical, mental, or emotional bandwidth necessary to offer every person we come in contact with a crash course in Grief Talk 101, nor is everyone open to instruction.

If it's possible, if they will hear it and if you are able to do so, there is nothing wrong with saying, "I'm sorry; that wasn't helpful." And explain why. If explaining isn't possible or won't be productive, thank them for their concern and change the subject or walk away.

The willingness to engage the conversation around death, loss, and grief in a positive way is emerging, but there is still a lot of work to do. At the present moment, one of the best options may be to lead by example. To continue to be who you are, where you are, how you are. To own and tell your truth—your story. That is the first step toward connection—to ourselves, to the Holy, and to one another—and connection is the first step toward healing.

When I kept it all inside, my bones turned to powder, my words
became daylong groans.
The pressure never let up; all the juices of my life dried up.
Psalm 32:3–4 MSG

Help Us Find the Words

The world is full of words, Holy One.
Help us find the right ones.
Words of grace, not accusation.
Words of acceptance, not rejection.
Words with space enough to hold more than one point of view.

Help us find the words that convey our hurt
without inflicting more pain,
words that speak of need and desire
without manipulating.

Help us find the words to address our anger
without inflaming or laying blame,
words that communicate our thoughts
without discounting others.

Help us find words that open the door to dialogue,
and keep us from slamming that door by insisting on the last word.
Help us find words that articulate our differences
with respect, not condemnation.

Help us find words that will draw the circle wide,
with room for all,
words that speak peace,
offer hope, share love.

Help us find the words—and the courage—
to speak our truth—and speak truth to power—when necessary,
to honestly name what is there
without hypocrisy or prejudice.

And hold our tongues when our words
would only harm or destroy.

Chapter 11

THERE IS A FINE LINE BETWEEN THE LEADING EDGE OF PROGRESS AND THE RAGGED EDGE OF DISASTER.

Invitation: Look beyond either/or.

My husband was a fly-by-the-seat-of-your-pants poster child, always looking for the next new thing to try. He was one of the first in our farming area to make the switch from traditional tillage to no-till farming in the early 1980s. We owned a state-of-the-art, computerized Weigh-Tronix feed mill that precisely portioned and mixed the individual ingredients in the various rations used in our farrow-to-finish hog operation. In 1999, he spent a week at the Harbor Branch Oceanographic Institute in Fort Pierce, Florida, investigating whether aquaculture was more economically viable than raising hogs, and that summer we had a four-hundred-gallon fish tank full of hybrid striped bass and crappie in our basement. Had NASA or SpaceX called and offered him a spot on the next launch into outer space, he would have gone without thinking twice. Always

looking ahead—and seeing possibility everywhere, in everything—
he thrived on the experimental, the innovative, the cutting edge. It
energized him, engaging his creativity at the most fundamental level.
It gave him life.

The ultimate techno-geek, he'd never met a gadget he didn't
like, although he found some more fun than others. Computers were
his favorite. He loved them so much he learned how to build his
own and in 2011 spent a week at a SANS Institute boot-camp-style
internet security conference I affectionately referred to as "hacker
school." After completing the class, he took and passed the GIAC
Security Essentials certification test and used that expertise to help
people, building and maintaining computer systems for others, including the library in the town where the church he served was lo-
cated, and he did it all *gratis*, just because he loved doing it.

That "What's new? What's next?" mindset was so much a part
of who he was, he faced his illness and approaching death the same
way. He asked a handful of questions during the initial hospital stay,
when we got the preliminary diagnosis, but once he saw the MRI
film with the location of the tumors and heard the biopsy results,
his focus shifted to the future. At the end of every visit, the hospice
nurses always asked if he had any questions. Only one: "Why am I
still here?" As soon as it was clear to him his physical life was ending,
he was ready to move on to the next part.

Psalm 116:15 reads, "Precious in the sight of the LORD is the
death of his saints" (RSV). In her *Psalms for Praying: An Invitation to
Wholeness* volume, Nan Merrill renders it this way: "Precious to

You are all who live in Love, who abandon themselves into your loving care."[15]

That's exactly what Bill did. For him, that terminal diagnosis was not a limited, life-or-death reality. It was both/and. The end of his earthly life was merely a transition—a bridge—to the next grand adventure, the Holy Grail of progress: heaven.

For me, it was the end of the world.

Plunged almost instantly (and completely unprepared) into widowhood was like being dropped into a foreign country where I didn't know anyone, didn't know the customs or the language, had no idea where I was, and had no clue where I was going or how to get there. I, the person who always had a plan, suddenly had no idea what to even plan for, and I had no idea how to plan for *that*. Firmly planted on the other side of that fine line, the ragged edge of disaster was where I lived.

Packing to move—disorienting and jarring by itself—intensified those feelings of disaster.

The very last things I packed before putting my suitcases in the car and heading for my new home—ironically, or not, on the one-year anniversary of the day he told me something might be wrong—was all that tech stuff he loved so much: computer, monitors (of course he had more than one), cables, software, surround-sound speakers, external hard drives, receiver, DVR, PS3, Wii—all the tangible, concrete symbols of his it's-the-adventure-of-the-thing personality.

---

15 Nan C. Merrill, *Psalms for Praying: An Invitation to Wholeness* (New York: Continuum, 1997), 246.

Touching the things that so defined his life and meant so much to him was (almost) like touching him again, but because of their intimate connection to him, they were also the things that reminded me most acutely of his absence and how much I missed him. Picking each one up, wrapping it, and placing it in a box unleashed emotional whiplash, that searing "head snap" sensation when your feelings turn on a dime, from comfort and joy to sorrow and loss, the bare desk where his computer once sat mirroring the hole in my heart and the emptiness of my life.

The ragged edge of disaster, indeed.

He always asked, "What else is possible?" He looked at every event and circumstance as challenge, invitation, opportunity. As his polar opposite, my first—often my only—question was, "What's wrong with this picture?" I focused first on what didn't—wouldn't—work, where the land mines were, the potential for failure. Convinced you could have only one or the other, I lived in an either/or world. You had progress or disaster; you could be happy or sad. Never both.

I was wrong.

Even in progress, there are elements of disaster. The old has to be dismantled, or at the very least reconfigured, in order to make way and create room for the new thing that is emerging.

Our existence is not a singular, either/or proposition. Life is full of both/ands of every shade and stripe. The world is at once beautiful and terrible. There is darkness and light, joy and sorrow, good and evil, faith and doubt, strength and weakness, right and wrong, order and chaos, war and peace, life and death. As Solomon so eloquently pointed out and the Byrds so beautifully sang, there are times and seasons for everything, and within those seasons are instances when those both/ands occur and coexist at the very same moment.

Understanding loss as part of the tapestry of my life, not a stand-alone event within an isolated sliver of time, helped me see beyond that ragged edge of disaster and embrace the fact that it is both possible and permissible to feel—at the same time—the fond memories I have of the one I love, the joy he brought to my life, *and* the pain of how much I miss him.

I didn't realize that on the night I packed up all that technology, all those things that defined and evoked memories of the person to whom I had my deepest human connection in the world. The loss— the ragged edge of disaster—was all I could see and where I was afraid I was always going to be. I wasn't able to acknowledge that *and* grasp and hang on to all the good, the love that was still resident in my heart and soul, in the midst of the aching loss and sorrow.

Embracing the both/and-ness of life also helps me weather that string of unhappy anniversaries that dot the calendar in June. Within the space of seven short days is sandwiched Bill's death, our wedding anniversary, the date of his visitation, and the day of his funeral.

The events and emotions of that time frame are seared into my consciousness. I can't forget, unsee, or unfeel them, and because they happen in such rapid succession, the effects are cumulative.

Years after the fact, it's still possible for me to lose it at ten minutes till four on June 12, no matter where I am or what I'm doing. Our physical connection ended with his last breath, and the memories of that life-shattering moment cannot be completely erased.

I can't always make it through dinner (or breakfast or lunch) on June 16, our anniversary, without tears; remembering the day our lives were joined together before God exacerbates the pain of living without him. Images of his casket and the cemetery dominate my consciousness on June 17 and 18, regardless of where I am or what I'm doing.

Culture's prescription for dealing with unhappy anniversaries is to not think about them. Culture preaches avoidance and does so in many guises, one of which is positive thinking: "Forget the bad stuff, focus on the good, and everything will be fine." We are expected to, as Monty Python put it in their song by the same name, "always look on the bright side of life," the implication being that if I don't—if I name what these days are for me, which is dark and painful, sad and difficult—I'm setting myself up for misery and guaranteeing that misery is all those days will ever be. Culture wants me to believe that openly acknowledging the elephant in the room—my grief—will automatically, by virtue of the fact that I articulated it, turn said elephant loose to trample on everything and make things even worse.

Not so.

It is not only possible to do both, but you can do so with honesty and integrity.

Life is exactly as those wedding vows we spoke on that June night in 1972 proclaim. It holds joy *and* sorrow, sickness *and* health, plenty *and* want. There is room for laughter amid the tears. We can—we should—have moments of joy even when we're grieving and experience gratitude and contentment even while mourning what we've lost.

Coming to the place where I am able to do that—to own some small measure of joy in the midst of the sadness; to entertain a fond memory; to hold the vision of one meaningful, beautiful thing—is what enables me to, as Jan Richardson says, "confront [the sorrow and loss] with healing, with transformation, with hope."[16]

Look the sadness in the face and feel it, but look also for beauty, joy, and love, and allow yourself to experience them without judgment or guilt. They are not mutually exclusive. Life—all of it, including grief and loss—is not either/or. It is always both/and.

And there was evening, and there was morning.
Genesis 1:5 NIV

---

16 Richardson, *In the Sanctuary of Women*, 257.

And . . .

So tiny, that word and—
and yet so powerful.

The lynchpin of Creation,
in that small word, and, *is unlimited possibility;*
space and time for all there is, all we are, all we do.

Light and darkness, evening and morning,
skies and heavens.
Land and sea, plants and animals,
sun and moon, shining stars.

Dust and breath, male and female,
times and seasons—every one.
Life and death, seedtime and harvest,
killing and healing.

Building up and tearing down, weeping and laughter,
mourning and dancing.

Gathering and scattering, embracing and refraining,
searching and losing.

Keeping and discarding, tearing and mending,
speech and silence,
love and hate, war and peace.

Remind me, Holy One, when my vision narrows,
when my view constricts, when I see things only one way,
that and—*that possibility*—*is the hallmark of Creation and is*
embedded in your every interaction with us, your creatures.

Help me see it always,
in all ways, in all things.

Help me live in the abundance of the and, *not the exclusion of the* or.

Chapter 12

THERE IS A FINE LINE BETWEEN KNOWING ABOUT SOMETHING AND HAVING IT ETCHED INTO YOUR LIFE AND EXPERIENCE.

Invitation: Name your truth.

I knew *about* death and dying and grief and grieving.

At least I thought I did.

The pastoral care course I took in the process of becoming certified as a lay pastor in the Presbyterian Church (U.S.A.) was taught by the head chaplain of one of the major medical centers near us and a registered nurse who had studied at the famed St. Christopher's Hospice in London, England; had founded the first hospice program in the Maritimes; and was (when I knew her) a tenured professor of medical humanities at the Southern Illinois University School of Medicine. Significant portions of the curriculum on death and dying she taught the medical students were also included in our classwork.

I'd been to multiple conferences and workshops on the topic that featured well-respected speakers: Dr. Ira Byock, at that time the president of the American Academy of Hospice and Palliative Medicine; the Rev. Dr. Tom Long, preaching professor and author of two books on the Christian funeral; and Dr. William Hoy, a medical humanities professor whose expertise is in the role of social support in death, dying, and grief.

One entire shelf of the bookcase in my church office was devoted to volumes on death, dying, grief, and loss from a wide range of perspectives, some authored by grieving parents, some by grieving spouses, some by pastors, and some by counselors and therapists. Some were written from a medical point of view, some from a pastoral care perspective, and some from a palliative care paradigm. There were even a couple penned by patients themselves, written as a way to come to terms with the potentially terminal diagnoses they'd been given.

In addition to all that book learning, I had plenty of what had passed, until my husband's death, for personal experience with grief and grieving. I'd regularly—far too regularly, it seemed—accompanied the parishioners I loved and served as they walked the labyrinth of loss, providing pastoral care and officiating close to a hundred funerals and memorial services in my more than twenty years of pastoral ministry.

That is not the same thing as making the trip yourself.

It isn't even close.

Not even the loss of immediate family members—my parents, brother, and in-laws—prepared me for the unexpected illness and death of my husband of forty-one years, 361 days.

Knowledge about something is vastly different from having those experiences etched into your personal, day-to-day consciousness. It's the difference between watching sports on TV and taking the field, the court, the track, or the course yourself. Rather than experiencing vicariously—as an observer, an onlooker—you are immersed in it, a full participant.

I felt the same emotions when Bill died as I had walking with others in their loss, but because our relationship was so much longer, deeper, and more intimate, my reactions were far more intense. I wasn't sad; I was inconsolable. My heart didn't just hurt; it was shattered. I had no idea how or why this happened or how to find out, no clue how to cope with that much pain, how to function when literally every facet of my existence had been upended, when everything I believed was being challenged, when all those things I had been oh-so-sure of disintegrated in front of me, when the very place I would have gone for comfort was now lost to me.

I bumped up against culture's understanding and ways of dealing with grief (spoiler alert: it doesn't deal with it) and what I thought I knew in constant and constantly painful ways. And that shelf full of grief books in my office turned out to be less than helpful. In the beginning, I simply wasn't able to read; I didn't have enough emotional energy to focus long enough to engage and process information. Later, when I could, I found little that resonated. Those books were truth for those who had written them, a record of their experience, but they weren't where and how I was.

Living into my own grief, which was vastly different from what culture portrays and what the books I owned described, dismantled everything I thought I knew.

I thought I should be able to manage my grief by myself. I had a master's degree in a social-work-type discipline; I'd taken all kinds of courses in helping skills and life span and developmental psychology. I was a pastor. I had those books. I had been to all those workshops. I should know what to do and have all the answers or be able to look them up. I, of all people, should not need any help.

I was wrong.

I couldn't do it by myself then, and can't do it by myself now. *And I'm not supposed to.* I need to befriend and tend myself, yes, but I also need the love and companionship of the Holy, and I need to surround myself with people who will walk with me, allow me to be where I am and how I am, who will encourage me and support me, who will bring light and life into my days.

I thought the first year would be the hardest and if I could just get through the next thing, whatever that was, life would get better—easier. It would all happen when Bill's illness had run its course; when "death was past and pain ended," as one of the prayers in my faith tradition's *Book of Common Worship* says; when the visitation and funeral were over; when the grave marker was set; when the estate paperwork was finished; when all those "lasts" and all the "firsts" (anniversary, Father's Day, birthday, holidays) had been endured and survived.

Wrong again.

The second milestones and anniversaries turned out to be even more painful than the firsts. Expecting the firsts to be difficult, I'd carefully considered and planned for them. I wasn't as intentional in the way I approached them the second time, erroneously thinking I'd "been there, done that, and had the closet full of T-shirts to prove it," and the unvarnished and unprepared-for intensity blindsided me.

Although culture tries to enforce one—albeit an extremely short one—there is no time line or schedule to grieving; no statute of limitations; no certain number of days, weeks, months, or years after which the emotions and tears subside.

I thought unless I was home alone, I had to hide my tears. Our "appearance is everything" world has no patience with anyone who appears to be less than their "practically perfect in every way" Mary Poppins best. I was afraid, especially with all the extra expectations I'd heaped on myself as a pastor, that if I cried in public, others would think me needy, unstable, unhinged. That I wasn't handling things "well."

Wrong again.

Tears are a natural response to grief, no matter who or where you are—not a sign of weakness or an inability to cope. They are healing and cleansing, a blessed release without which our sorrow would consume us. There's no timetable for that either. Healing is always possible, ever ongoing, which means tears can occur any time, any place.

I thought it would be the big-ticket things—holidays and all those unhappy anniversaries—that would regularly leave me sobbing. Those watershed events *are* difficult, and I do cry, but not over all of them and not every time.

The little things, things so seemingly inconsequential they aren't even on my radar, often affect me the deepest. Fascinating, unpredictable, often debilitating—the triggers of grief are everywhere, and they strike with unfathomable randomness.

Any cue or memory can prompt sorrow and tears: Catching a whiff of the Cool Water cologne Bill always wore when I'm out running errands. Baseball. He was a die-hard Cubs fan. When they won the World Series in 2016 after a 108-year drought, most fans were delirious with joy. I wept for days, dissolving every time I heard or talked about it. Digging through a file folder and finding papers with his handwriting on them. Baking a pie—his favorite dessert and what he requested for his last birthday (which none of us realized it would be at the time) rather than cake. Standing on my front porch watching a SpaceX rocket scream through the sky. He loved space and everything about it. Catching sight of the spacecraft instantly brings those memories—and the pain of missing him—flooding back.

Avoiding triggers, which is culture's advice, sounds preferable, admirable even. "Don't suffer needlessly. Just don't go there." But that isn't possible in the real world. And as marriage and family therapist Vienna Pharaon says, it doesn't work anyway:

> Avoiding your triggers isn't healing. Healing happens when you're triggered and you're able to move through the pain, the pattern, and the story, and walk away to a different ending.[17]

I thought I knew about grief and grieving. But you can't think your way out of the sadness and pain. In order to live into the rest of my life, I had to let go of everything I thought I knew and name what was actually there—what was true for me, where I was, how I felt.

---

17 This quote appeared on her website, as of the printing of this book, at http://www.newyorkcouplescounseling.com/virtual-offerings/.

It was hard. Already feeling isolated and "other," going against culture's dictates made me feel even more lost and alone. And the fear factor was huge. I was terrified that by naming what was there, I would be letting the genie out of the bottle and my grief would overwhelm me.

It seems counterintuitive, but in fact the opposite is true.

When I finally allowed myself to name what was, my experience bore out what the biblical record says and what scientific research and Ignatian spirituality teach: there is power in naming.

"The name of the LORD is a strong tower," Solomon says in Proverbs 18:10 (RSV). "Some trust in chariots and some in horses, but we trust in the name of the LORD our God," David insists in Psalm 20:7 (NIV). There are countless admonishments from Joel to Revelation to "call on *the name of the Lord*" (emphasis mine), implying that there is inherent power in the name itself to accomplish what is being asked.

Naming something conveys power and authority. It bestows identity. Once you know what something is, you can figure out how to deal with it. Naming those things that cause us pain, if only to ourselves, brings them out of the shadows and into the open, where they can be dealt with. It puts flesh on them, giving them a shape and form that enables us to engage and process them.

Everything we can't, won't, or don't name is free to maintain its fearful grip on us. Naming essentially declaws it.

Name your truth.

This is what the LORD says . . . :

"Call to me and I will answer you and tell you
great and unsearchable things you do not know."

Jeremiah 33:2–3 NIV

A Prayer for Naming

I come to you, Name above all Names,
you who know me by name and everything about me.
Help me look my life in the eye, Holy One,
and call what's there by its real name.

No sidestepping, no candy coating,
no avoidance, no denial,
just truth.

Give me the courage and the strength to articulate—
and face—the sorrow, confusion, and fear,
the weariness, frustration, and doubt,
the anger, the jealousy, the shadow side of me.

To welcome it all into the open,
give it a seat at the table,
learn to converse and live with it.

Just as you welcome me
and everything about me.

Part IV

TAKEAWAYS

The path to the labyrinth's center often bestows immediate benefits: a change of scenery, space and time to think, physical movement. Equally as important as those things we receive in the moment are the things we take with us back into the world. While not always a source of instant solutions or healing (although those things sometimes happen) the labyrinth experience offers gifts—grace, peace, understanding, emotional release, insight, and clarity—that continue to unfold and be made manifest in us.

An apt teacher, if we're willing to engage it, grief is rife with ongoing lessons and insights into who we are, where we fit in the world, and what we are called to do. There is, within the brokenness, opportunity—for restoration, redemption, transformation, resurrection. Step by step, we can pick up the pieces of our shattered existence and use that raw material to rebuild our lives.

Chapter 13

THERE IS A FINE LINE BETWEEN WORN AND WORN OUT.

Invitation: Be real.

I love the home I purchased and the sunny, warm-almost-all-year-round central Florida climate I relocated to, but there were some rocky days early on. In addition to the upheaval inherent in moving, I spent much of those first few weeks fraught with angst every time I walked through the house, worried I would irreparably damage my red oak hardwood floors. While beautiful, they show every scuff, scratch, ding, and speck.

The marks on the floor became a thorn in my side, one more reminder—not that I needed one—of all the things in my life that were broken, in disarray, not the way I wanted them and that life—especially mine, at that moment—was not perfect.

But life was not perfect before Bill's illness and death either, and it was never going to be. Even if my husband were alive today, our lives would not be without discomfort, sorrow, and loss. Sad and tragic stuff would still happen and would have to be dealt with.

I regarded them as symbols of defeat, but the scratches and scrapes on my floors—and in my life—do not render them ruined, worn out, or unserviceable. Underneath those marks, beyond them, in spite of them, and within those imperfections is the stuff of real life. They are patina—the *Velveteen Rabbit* thing:

> "Real isn't how you are made," said the Skin Horse. "It's a thing that happens to you. . . . Generally, by the time you are Real, most of your hair has been loved off, and your eyes drop out and you get loose in the joints and very shabby. But these things don't matter at all, because once you are Real you can't be ugly, except to people who don't understand."[18]

I didn't understand in the beginning. But I learned.

What I needed to embrace was not the Minwax touch-up pen or the Bona mop and floor cleaner. It was the fact that my floors are a visible incarnation of the opportunity and the potential for new life. *Real* life.

Perfection isn't the point.

Real is what matters. Living authentically and well.

This is my home, not a hotel, which, by necessity, has to appear perfect to and for every guest. *I live here. Life happens here.* And life—real life—is messy, full of dents and dings, foibles and fracases, populated with all manner of brokenness, incompletion, and imperfection, including loss and grief, dripping blood, sweat, and tears.

---

18 Margery Williams, *The Velveteen Rabbit* (New York: Doubleday, 1922, 1991), 5–6.

Culture treats those things as I did my floors, as something un-serviceable and in need of repair. The unspoken message—because negative things, particularly death, loss, and grief, are not openly discussed—is that you need to fix it and move on, and the sooner, the better. It sounds deceptively simple and like what we think we want, but it doesn't work because grief isn't a repair project. Parker Palmer says it straight up: "The human soul doesn't want to be advised or fixed or saved. It simply wants to be witnessed—to be seen, heard and companioned exactly as it is."[19]

Physical things like damaged houses and cars and my floors can be returned to their pre-disaster condition, but for us human creatures, loss, trauma, and pain weave themselves into the fabric of our lives. They become part of who we are. They can't be undone, erased, plastered over, or otherwise made to disappear.

But they can be built on.

In her chapter on the new model of grief in her book *It's OK That You're Not OK*, Megan Devine says, "The new model of grief is not in cleaning it up and making it go away; it's in finding new and beautiful ways to inhabit what hurts."[20]

The answer is not to, as the Servpro people put it, make it "like it never even happened." In the brokenness of our lives—the pain, the flaws, the shards of what's left—is opportunity, an invitation to pick up the pieces, and like the Japanese art of kintsugi and the age-old crafts of mosaic and quilting, use them as the raw material for rebuilding our lives.

19 Parker J. Palmer, "The Gift of Presence, The Perils of Advice," *On Being* (blog), April 27, 2016, https://onbeing.org/blog/the-gift-of-presence-the-perils-of-advice/.
20 Megan Devine, *It's OK That You're Not OK: Meeting Grief and Loss in a Culture That Doesn't Understand* (Boulder, CO: Sounds True, 2017), 60.

Coming to this understanding has changed more than just my attitude toward my floors. My perception of what it means and what it takes to be real—to live authentically and well—has evolved too.

It was ingrained in me early in life to reserve the best things—the good china, the "nice" clothes, fancy meals—for special occasions, never for everyday use.

I get it. Ritual and symbolism matter. Making sure there are special things to mark those special days imparts meaning, which is hugely important. But having lost Bill far too soon and so unexpectedly, I live daily with the realization burned into my bones that tomorrow isn't promised to any of us. Today is what we have, and each day of life is a gift of grace from the hand of the Creator, which, for no other reason than that, deserves to be celebrated in some manner.

I recall with deep regret the bottle of 1994 Opus One wine Bill and I were saving for some special occasion. We talked many times about drinking it—for our twenty-fifth anniversary, our thirtieth, our thirty-fifth, our fortieth, when our son returned from Kuwait—but we never did, always opting to leave it cellared for some other, more important occasion down the road. One that never arrived.

I finally opened it four days after his death, on what would have been our forty-second wedding anniversary, and I'm eternally sorry I missed sharing it with him.

I had no idea how precious even the everyday days were until my husband was no longer physically present to share them with me.

Now I do, and I do things differently.

I don't hoard special things for special occasions that may never arrive. I'll get out my grandmother's celery dish for a simple Friday night dinner or use my mom's Fostoria American platter and bowl for veggies and dip on Super Bowl Sunday. My grandkids know, without asking, that it's perfectly okay to grab a crystal goblet for their milk, juice, or Gatorade. I live close enough to make spur-of-the-moment trips to Disney World, and I do. Instead of always waiting for someday, as I used to, I try to focus on living well today. That includes both embracing what is, no matter how broken and painful, and using the "good stuff," bringing some level of celebration into everyday life.

We did it sometimes. I recall one Friday night in particular when Bill and I sat at our kitchen table eating carryout pizza out of the box by candlelight, drinking a $6 bottle of wine out of Lenox glasses. We didn't do it nearly enough.

No matter how much of a shambles—how unserviceable—my life appears to me, in the kingdom of heaven, nothing is useless or wasted. Those less-than-perfect things in our lives—our brokenness, our pain, our flaws—are not singularly negative, nor do they put the Sacred off. Rather, they flame the desire of the One who made us and loves us without end to draw us close, and they are the raw material from which the Holy One can fashion our redemption, our re-creation, our restoration, our resurrection.

Don't wait for that perfect moment that may never come. Love big. Celebrate daily. Give generously. Use the good china. Or paper plates. Drink the good wine. Make real coffee. Buy some flowers. Have the chocolate. Write that love note.

Live authentically and well. Be real.

> I have loved you with an everlasting love;
> I have drawn you with unfailing kindness.
> I will build you up again, and you . . . will be rebuilt.
> Jeremiah 31:3–4 NIV

Abundant and Real

When I look at the landscape of my life, Holy One,
what I see is broken. Painful. Incomplete.
Stumbling blocks.

But offered to you, infused with your Spirit,
they become building blocks.

The ultimate Recycler, nothing in my life
or in your kingdom
is useless or wasted.

Restoration, redemption, resurrection, becoming
are not only always possible,
they are the order of the day,
this day and every day.

Open my eyes, Sacred Presence,
to the love, the grace, the abundance
all around me,
and help me embrace and walk in it.

May creativity and celebration
fill my days,
the peaceful slumber of
hours well lived mark my nights.

Chapter 14

THERE IS A FINE LINE BETWEEN "I'VE NEVER DONE IT THAT WAY BEFORE!" AND "SURE. WHY NOT?"

Invitation: Do new things in new ways.

In the southeastern United States, wearing sunglasses is not a luxury or merely a fashion statement. It is a necessity. In the tropics, the sun—which shines almost every day, almost all day long—is relentless, so everyone from infants to ninety-somethings wear sunglasses. They are the last thing I grab, along with my keys, my phone, and a bottle of water, when I leave the house each morning for my three-or-so-mile walk. (One of the last things my husband made me promise him, when he could still speak intelligibly, was that I would take care of myself. I'm doing my best to honor that; hence, the daily walk.)

I usually take the same route every day for two very good reasons. First, as I've mentioned before (like, maybe a million times), I'm a creature of habit with a bent toward organization. My brain is hardwired that way, and that's the default strategy I use to cope: drag everything out into the open and pick through it piece by piece, sorting, categorizing, labeling (and discarding when necessary), until you reach a point where you can make sense of what you have left; then put it all back where it belongs. I find the combination of physical activity plus mental engagement therapeutic. It doesn't work for everything, but it works for a lot of things, not just in the tangible, physical world, but in the emotional and spiritual realms as well.

That morning walk gives me the opportunity to thoroughly assess my circumstances, not just pay lip service to what is going on in my life. It allows me time to mentally unpack and sort out what I really think and how I really feel, to address issues; to discard thought processes and emotional responses that are not positive or productive; to come to conclusions; to make decisions; and, finally, because as I walk I also pray, to intentionally hand it all over to the One who loves me without end, an offering of my whole self, laid on the altar of God's grace.

Second, because of the way the neighborhood is laid out, taking the same route every morning affords me the shortest amount of time spent walking into the blazing morning sun. My husband's standard operating procedure was to put off doing those things he was not enthusiastic about for as long as possible, in hopes that perhaps he would not have to do them at all. My modus operandi is the exact opposite: do the least pleasant things first, get them out of the way, and then you have the rest of the day—or week!—to do things you enjoy, or at least enjoy more than whatever was at the top of the to-do list. So every day, I walk east and south first, get it over with, and then move on to the more pleasant phase of the walk.

There is great value in taking a good, long look at what is in front of you, calling it by its real name, and dealing with it head-on. But just like the fact that without sunglasses, the morning sun crosses the line from illuminating to blinding, there are times when full-frontal reality is just too much to bear. There were many days when being face-to-face with the details of my now-changed-forever existence crossed that line, when it pierced my soul and became overwhelming. I devolved to what I knew, to what I always used to do. But since every detail in my life was now different, that didn't work the way it used to.

There comes a point in everyone's life when it is simply not possible to keep doing the things you've always done the way you've always done them.

I understand—at a level I previously had no frame of reference for—the collective angst of church sessions, councils, vestries, and boards everywhere who, when change—or even just the *possibility* of change—is visited upon them, lament, "But we've never done it that way before!"

With the love of my life no longer physically present in my life, this is where I live. Nothing is the way it was. Every single minute of every single day is an adventure in "I've never done it this way before!"

It is an overwhelmingly uncomfortable and scary place to live. So unsure is this territory, I had difficulty trusting my judgment and stepping into all these new-for-me areas—even on my morning walk.

But one day I did it.

I walked out the front door, and instead of going south and east, I turned north and west.

The sunlight strikes everything in different places when you change direction 180 degrees. Instead of being in my face, it warmed my back. Rather than having to squint through the first mile or so (even while wearing sunglasses!), I was able to open my eyes and take in the details of my surroundings. Come to find out, the north and west loop of the circle I live on is longer; by the time I did turn east and south, the sun was high enough in the sky that it wasn't burning directly into my eyeballs.

It was the same neighborhood. The same cars were in the same driveways; the same people were walking the same dogs; the same landscaping crews mowed the grass the same day every week. But with a 180-degree change in vantage point, things looked different.

I didn't have any grand epiphanies that day. There was no huge tectonic shift in the inner landscape of my life. The puzzle pieces of my existence (which are still many) did not all fall instantly into place. I would not say I returned to the house feeling exhilarated. But wisps of possibility, where I could see none before, seemed to be floating in the air.

Is that what the leading edge of progress feels like? Might I have felt the barest hint, gotten the smallest taste, taken the babiest of steps toward that place of optimism and hope my husband lived in every day?

I think so.

The current of tradition and familiarity runs deep. The pull is strong and difficult to swim against because the observance of tradition is one of the ways we human creatures lay claim to our identity. Observing traditions—engaging in intentional acts at specific times and places—affirms for us and for the rest of the world, "This is who we are, and this is what we do." That sense of belonging that comes from knowing who we are and what we do affords us no small measure of comfort.

But whether by slow evolution over the arc of our lives or in instantaneous or unexpected corporate or personal events like my husband's untimely death, our lives don't ever remain static, nor can the status quo be preserved in any "dragonflies in amber" sort of way.

Even when the hallmark of our lives is consistency—when we live in the same locality, in the same house, with the same people, do the same work, attend the same church, belong to the same organizations, and cherish the same values over our entire lifetime—time and circumstances still change us.

Stuff happens. Or doesn't. Things both big and small impact who we are, how we feel, what we think, what we do. Just one good night's sleep or one bad one can significantly alter our perception, mood, mindset, creativity, energy, activity level, and schedule.

Some traits—the core essence of who we are—remain constant over the course of our lifetime, but we're not exactly the same people we were last year or last month or even last week. We learn, we grow, we mature, we evolve, we adapt, and at times the things we do and the way we do them have to adapt and change as well.

The question is not what we do *if* things change but what we do *when* things change, and that involves doing things we've never done before and doing things in new and different ways.

> See, I am doing a new thing!
> Isaiah 43:19 NIV

New

I want so much to know, Holy One,
to be sure of who I am,
where I'm going, where I fit in the world.

But clinging to the comfortable, the familiar,
the way I've always done it
leaves my fists clenched,
my fingers closed around what was,
unable to open and receive what is, what can be, and what will be.

Pry them open, Loving Presence,
my hands, my eyes, my heart.

Fashion in me wells and hollows,
caverns and crevices,
where your creative Spirit
can flow through, can wash over, can seep in,
bringing light, renewal, re-creation, joy.

Chapter 15

THERE IS A FINE LINE BETWEEN GETTING THERE AND BEING THERE.

Invitation: Be present.

*E*lisabeth Kübler-Ross's work on death and dying was ground-breaking. She chose to shine a light on something that few are willing to talk about even now. But her conclusions have not been without controversy. There are indeed stages to death, dying, and their concomitant partners, grief and grieving. What is problematic is the erroneous perception held by some that it is a linear process. It is anything but, and in her *On Grief and Grieving* volume, she says so herself:

> The stages have evolved since their introduction, and they have been very misunderstood over the past three decades. They were never meant to help tuck messy emotions into neat packages. They are responses to loss that many people have,

but there is not a typical response to loss, as there is no typical loss. Our grief is as individual as our lives.

The five stages—denial, anger, bargaining, depression, and acceptance—are a part of the framework that makes up our learning to live with the one we lost. They are tools to help us frame and identify what we may be feeling. But they are not stops on some linear timeline in grief. Not everyone goes through all of them or goes in a prescribed order.[21]

But, boy, did I want to.

I wanted it to work that way because planning and organization are hardwired into my DNA. That's the way *I* work. There was already a list! Stages and steps! I wanted to start at the top, go item by item—in order, of course—and, as Larry the Cable Guy says, "Git-r-done!" I wanted to "get there" and get on with the rest of my life.

It didn't work for two reasons.

First, that's not the way grief works.

Defying any attempt to quantify and categorize, grief follows no time lines or schedules. It can't be reduced to or contained in a collection of items on a list or points on a map. There is no one-way, nonstop flight. No AAA TripTik Travel Planner that will guide you from point A to point B while avoiding all the construction zones, toll roads, and speed traps. There is a path, but grief is as personal as it is universal; each of us has to find and follow our own.

---

21 Elisabeth Kübler-Ross and David Kessler, *On Grief and Grieving: Finding the Meaning of Grief Through the Five Stages of Loss* (New York: Scribner, 2005), 7.

Nor, as Kübler-Ross herself affirmed, is the process linear in any way. Grief meanders here and there, in and around, with more twists and turns than a Quentin Tarantino film or a theme park roller coaster—or a labyrinth.

Just like, "There's no crying in baseball," as Tom Hanks's character, Jimmy Dugan, insists in the movie *A League of Their Own,* there's no "getting there" in grief. It isn't a destination you arrive at and depart from. It's part of life—ongoing, lived-into experience.

The second reason "getting there" didn't work was because I had no idea where I was going—what the rest of my life was supposed to look like—and no clue how to figure it out.

Even without the overwhelming emotion and fog of grief, visualizing and charting the future is tough for me. Finite, concrete scenarios are minimally manageable; I suck at long-term planning.

When I married Bill, I hitched my wagon to an eternal optimist of the highest order who spent every waking moment searching for the next new thing, entertaining any and every scenario, and seeing endless possibility in all of it. He did more than enough visioning for both of us; I never had to learn.

Once a goal is achieved or a project completed, I can backtrack and explain, in minute detail, exactly how I accomplished it. In the moment, I've got nothing. I could not complete the outline for my master's thesis—usually done first—until I'd finished writing. During my days as a pastor, I rarely came up with that snappy sermon title before crafting it, and sometimes not until after I'd preached it.

The bigger the picture and the higher the stakes, the faster the tiniest smidgen of uncertainty panics me. Stuck on the hamster wheel of what-ifs, I bathe each thought in fear-laden questions in the same manner one would baste a Thanksgiving turkey. (In my mind's eye, I can see my husband in the background, shaking his head and yelling, "Stop already! For the love of God, *just put down the spoon!*")

There was nothing bigger or more high stakes for me than trying to navigate the landscape of my life without the love of my life, my confidant, soulmate, and best friend. Trying to wrap my head around what to do and how was impossible. I. Couldn't. Even.

I wandered long in that "I don't know where I'm going, and I don't know how to get there!" wilderness before I was introduced to the practice of discernment and realized, as I began to engage in it, that it's not about "getting there"; it's about *being* there. Noticing. Being present and allowing myself to experience what is and what is happening, both in and around me.

Bill and I traveled to Amsterdam in 2006. It was an incredible trip, one of the highlights of our life together, but not everything was idyllic and perfect. There were broken airplanes and lost hotel reservations. Jet lag and the exhaustion that accompanies it are real things, and they are not fun. Winding up sick enough to need a doctor in a foreign country—and one of us was—is a nightmare. The beautiful lobby of the Hotel De Bilderberg—a must-see, we were told—was a tarp-shrouded construction zone while we were there, as was the Rijksmuseum, where much of the country's fine art is housed; we were only able to tour one wing.

It was still amazing, and the joy in that trip, everything we learned about each other and ourselves, was made flesh, real, tangible—was woven into our beings—within the process of the journey, in all the things we saw and experienced and shared along the way. It wasn't about getting there. It was about *being* there—being present every moment and fully experiencing everything that happened.

In his book *The Art of Pilgrimage*, Phil Cousineau writes, "It's the *process* . . . that leads us to the truth of our evolving journey."[22] He was speaking particularly about writing in that section, but I believe the concept holds true in many areas of our lives, including grief and loss.

Not a destination, not a one-and-done proposition, not something you fix, recover from, or get over, grief and loss are part of life, part of the human story, and we all experience various types of them. We lose loved ones, pets, car keys, basketball games. We lose jobs, houses, our health. We lose patience, our tempers, innocence, trust. We lose our grip, our mind, our way. Faith can be shaken, vows broken, relationships disintegrated. We lose our sense of safety and security in the wake of tragic events, political upheaval, and natural disasters.

The details of our particular losses are part of our personal story, all of which need to be acknowledged and mourned in an appropriate way. Unless we face, name, own, and articulate those things, there are gaps and holes in our existence that are unexplored and untended, significant portions of our lives left shrouded in mystery.

22 Phil Cousineau, *The Art of Pilgrimage: The Seeker's Guide to Making Travel Sacred* (Berkeley, CA: Conari Press, 1998), 113.

Being present to our grief is excruciating—and excruciatingly hard work. But it is in bearing witness, in experiencing and being present to what is happening to us and in us, that the way opens for insight, understanding, and healing to come, bit by bit, piece by piece, step by step.

It's not about getting there; it's about *being* there.

Wherever you are, whatever you're going through, be present.

Be still, and know.

Psalm 46:10 NIV

On Being

Reorient me, gracious God.
Draw me into your presence,
that I may be present.

Not distracted by what might happen down the road,
not bound, still, by what has already come and gone,
but here, now.

Deliver me from pie-in-the-sky thinking
that takes no account of my present reality.
Keep me also from clinging to
what I thought were "the good old days."

Keep me present, Creator God,
to what is,
present to what is happening, how I feel,
to my thoughts, my body, my surroundings.

Present most of all, Holy One, to you,
face to face, eye to eye, heart to heart,
aware always of the gifts of your presence:
Companionship. Rest. Courage. Comfort.
Constancy. Peace. Love.

Chapter 16

THERE'S A FINE LINE BETWEEN PONDERING AND SHEER AVOIDANCE.

Invitation: It is what it is. Embrace it.

At its heart, grief is a dance of engagement, of treading those fine lines, noticing the feelings they generate and all the other things they are wrapped up in and point to. Navigating it well requires participation, entering into, being present. Painful by its very nature, that engagement—walking the labyrinth of loss—is not easy, whether it's done with others or by ourselves. And it's further complicated by a culture that actively shies away from death and dying, grief and grieving.

Because grief is so painful, our natural human response is to want to spend as little time with it as possible. The temptation to deny its existence, shove it aside, pretend it's not there, is very real. We're actively encouraged by what culture says—and especially by what it doesn't—to discount and downplay.

I did it too.

My mantra, once we learned Bill's diagnosis and got a clear picture of what it entailed, became "It is what it is." His illness came from so far out of left field and so suddenly, I was in a state of total disbelief. I had to constantly remind myself that it was actually happening, that my reality had turned on a dime and nothing from that moment on was going to be the way I thought or expected things to be.

But I also used it to avoid.

The evening of Bill's biopsy, the staff nurse in the neuro intensive care unit called me to the desk to make sure we knew the schedule for visiting hours and to make me aware of things the medical team had been discussing that she wasn't sure Bill could comprehend or remember. His cognitive decline was already accelerating, and the anesthesia from the procedure further hindered his recall and ability to respond coherently.

We knew enough about Bill's illness to know it was awful. The nurse knew exactly what a glioblastoma diagnosis meant and how short life expectancy was for him, since the doctors had already ruled out surgery as a treatment option: too many tumors in too many places. To help, she made a list of resources I might want to look into. When she got to the information about CaringBridge, she choked up. "I'm so, so sorry," she said, tears streaming.

"It is what it is," I said. "Stuff happens, and we don't get to choose which stuff."

"You are amazing," she said. "If I were in your place, I would be freaking out right now. You're so strong!"

No, I wasn't. I was freaking out on the inside.

But I couldn't allow myself to admit it, not even to a medical professional who understood every single thing about what we were facing and was offering help.

I was afraid if I gave voice to all of the things I was feeling—the fear, the anger, the disbelief, the loss I already knew was coming, the serious doubts I had about whether I could handle this—I was going to be sobbing hysterically in seconds. I didn't want to disrupt the entire ICU, and I didn't want to cause additional concern for my kids. With their dad's terminal diagnosis, they had more than enough to deal with already. I didn't want them worrying about me too.

I marshaled every single shred of emotional energy I had left and simply refused to go there.

"It is what it is." End of conversation.

I kept saying it as Bill's illness progressed because it let everybody off the hook. People would ask how things were, how he was, how I was. "It is what it is," I would say with a shrug. It was enough to acknowledge that, yes, this is a thing—*a really big thing*—but it also made clear the fact that there is nothing we can do about it, so there's no point in discussing it. It spared both me and whomever I was talking to from struggling to converse further about something for which neither of us had words.

"It is what it is" is an acknowledgment of reality, and it's so, so important to name that, but we can't stop there. Without engagement and intention, those words can trap us on the wrong side of that fine line between pondering and avoidance, holding us hostage to the status quo and keeping us from living into the rest of our lives in a meaningful way.

If we're not careful, "It is what it is" can come to mean "This is *all* it is, all it's ever going to be."

While much of what I heard, read, and thought I knew about grief and loss were not true for me, one thing was: life goes on.

We either choose to live it or not.

In his blessing "For Absence" in his book *To Bless the Space Between Us*, John O'Donohue writes, "May you be generous in your embrace of loss."[23]

Culture conditions us to not even acknowledge grief and loss, let alone embrace them. Culture actively encourages us to run the other way.

For a long time, I did.

Even when grief occupied nearly all of my time and attention, I can't say I regarded it *generously.*

But I should have.

It sounds confounding—an oxymoron—to apply the phrase *generous embrace* to grief and loss, but our contemporary understanding of the word *generous* as "unselfish" or "plentiful" didn't come about until the 1600s.[24] At its root, in addition to meaning "to clasp in the arms," *embrace* means "to handle; to cope with." [25]

23 John O'Donohue, *To Bless the Space Between Us: A Book of Blessings* (New York: Convergent Books, 2008), 45.

24 *Online Etymology Dictionary*, s.v. "generous," accessed November 2, 2020, https://www.etymonline.com/word/generous.

25 *Online Etymology Dictionary*, s.v. "embrace, accessed November 2, 2020, https://www.etymonline.com/word/embrace.

To be generous in my embrace of loss, to me, means this: It means engaging and paying attention to loss, whatever its source. It's part of the tapestry of my life, part of who I am and will become, and as such it deserves my respect. It means doing that which will help me cope. It means choosing life.

I wish I had been willing to embrace it sooner. That very first night in the neuro ICU. While I wanted to protect my kids, in reality there was nothing I could do (or not do) that would keep them from worrying about me. Nothing that would take away their pain, change the circumstances, alter the outcome.

It is what it is.

But it is not the only thing.

I would never have chosen it and still wish, a million times over, it never happened to me—especially as early as it did—yet the drastic changes in my existence that being widowed has brought about have led me to places and things that never would have been part of my experience any other way. I see things I never would have noticed before. I understand myself—who I am, and what I have to offer the world—in ways I never would have otherwise. I've done things I never would have done had this not happened to me when it did. Were Bill still physically present and sharing daily life with me, with his "it's the adventure of the thing" mindset, we would have been so busy going places and so deeply invested in that next new thing he'd seen on the horizon, whatever it was, I would never have had or taken the time to start a blog or write a book. It just wouldn't have happened.

Something else happened instead, and here I am.

It is what it is. And when I was willing to embrace it, it wound up being more than I ever thought it would or could be.

Don't misunderstand. I'm not saying losing Bill and being widowed is good. It's not. I hate it and pretty much everything about it. But even in that considerably less-than-perfect circumstance I would never have chosen had it been up to me, I have learned so much, and I would never have learned those things any other way.

I will never love loss, sorrow, or grief in any warm, fuzzy fashion. We will never be BFFs. But our acquaintance is intimate, deep, and ongoing. When grief visits—and it does; it will—I endeavor to treat it well, to be generous in my embrace, to engage it fully, to get my hands on it and grapple with it, to be open to what it has to teach me, to gratefully accept whatever gifts and wisdom it may impart.

Instead of refusing to look or shoving what's there under the rug or to the back burner, as I walk the labyrinth of loss these days, I more often greet my grief with questions: "What do you have to teach me today? This is how I feel; what is behind this particular emotion? This is what I see; what else is here? This is where I am; where might I be headed?"

I can't offer you a happily-ever-after ending or a step-by-step how-to for navigating grief and loss. Happily ever after only exists in fairy tales and movies, and there is no ending when it comes to grief. I live with it, walking the labyrinth of loss, every day. But life goes on.

Grief and loss do not have the last or the only word, and regardless of what we encounter on the path, we do not walk alone. When the storms of life come—be they tidal waves of grief, scorching tempers, desolations of spirit, unwelcome changes, physical illnesses, economic ruin, wind, fire, or flood—when disaster strikes, when there is nothing else left, when life as we have known it is over, the Holy is still there.

It is what it is. Embrace it generously.

> But Mary treasured up all these things
> and pondered them in her heart.
>
> Luke 2:19 NIV

A Litany of Thanksgiving

God of sunrise and sunset, praise and lament, life and death,
Thank you for awareness—even when what I am most aware of is pain.
In acknowledging—in naming and calling it out—
it can be offered for healing.

Thank you for vision—even when the view is not
what I want to see, nothing I would choose.
With vision—truly seeing—comes the opportunity for learning,
for gaining understanding, for cultivating wisdom.

Thank you for raw emotion—
the "not nice" stuff no one wants to exhibit or feel.
It reveals and brings me face-to-face with what is,
not just what I want—and want others—to see,
and asks me to pay attention.

Thank you for those misfit feelings of restlessness,
disquiet, discontent, confusion, uncertainty.
They are—if I allow them to be—
the drumbeat that drives my heart and soul
until I find my rest, my Source, my purpose, my life, in you.

Thank you for dependence
and for the opportunities and gifts it brings:
a season to be, without nonstop, excessive doing,
the fostering of companionship, cooperation,
collaboration, and community as I learn to ask for
what I need and offer what I can to others in need.

Thank you for questions that confuse and confound.
In the sifting and sorting of them,
in the sitting with and the listening to them,
emerges a sense of what is most important for me to tend to now—
what I need to hold close and what I need to let go.

Thank you for brokenness and lament
and the tears that accompany them.
They empty and cleanse; open me to
healing and comfort, light and love;
and bring with them the ability
to reach out with compassion and understanding
to others who are shattered and broken.

Thank you for brutal honesty.
Though painful, it clears the air, brings clarity, dispels illusion.
It holds the potential to unbind and set free.

Thank you, Holy One, that your ear is ever and always
attuned to the cries of our hearts,
be they joyful shouts of celebration, songs of praise,
or the gut-wrenching sobs of grief and despair.

Thank you that you are constantly working
in and through all things
for our redemption, our restoration, our healing,
and that you do so always with great, great love.

AFTERWORD

*I*t's been a while. As I write this, it has been more than six years since Bill's death.

Some things are very much the same: I still love him. I still miss him every single second of every single day. And he is still very much a part of my life, even without being physically present. I'm still a mom and grandma. And although I do it long-distance now, I'm still involved in our farming operation.

Some things are very different: I left the Midwest—where I'd spent my entire life—and relocated to Florida, trading fall colors, tornadoes, and blizzards for endless summer, humidity, and hurricanes. And after more than twenty-five years of living apart from my children, we're now all in the same place and can enjoy seeing each other not just on occasional holiday visits. We have dinner together every Friday night and breakfast each Sunday morning. It's glorious.

Some things are both: I'm finally doing what my husband always wanted me to do. The day job is no more; I'm a writer, not a pastor. But I still strive to craft words that are filled with grace and peace, life and hope, words that remind us of God's lavish and unending love for each one of us, words that draw us into the embrace of the Holy One.

I've learned much about grief, and it was nothing like what I thought I knew. While loss is universal, each loss is different, and rather than something to get over or a problem that needs to be fixed or solved, it becomes part of who we are, an ongoing, lived-into experience, like the circular, continuous path of the labyrinth.

And in the labyrinth, I found both a spiritual practice and a framework within which I could continue to process my grief.

It is my hope that in sharing my story, I've held space for and given you permission to face and name, to feel and articulate the hard places—the griefs and losses—in yours.

Tribal Talk

Original poem by William D. Swaar, circa 2011

The grievers gather slowly,
The words start hushed and low.
Then volume rises and below
starts the heartbeat of words.

Like a roaring surf it soars and falls,
but constant is the heartbeat of love and life and loss,
The baby's cry and the muffled sob
all a part of the steady rhythm.

Finally the room is hushed
While the sacred words are told.
Lives remembered, hope expressed,
Faith put on over fear.

ACKNOWLEDGMENTS

I have the same love/hate relationship with acknowledgments that lots of other writers do. This was such a journey of the heart for me, I absolutely want to name those who helped me bring this book to life. And I am terrified of forgetting someone. But, here goes.

Without my husband, Bill, this book would not exist. I almost typed, "I wish he could see it," but, of course, he has. Looking down from his eternal vantage point and carried with me as I wrote—always in my heart and on my mind—he is as much a part of the finished product as I am. *See, honey? I did it! I quit my day job and wrote. And I am still supporting your farming habit!*

Nor could I have done this without the encouragement, love, and support of my son, Matt; my daughter, Lisa; and their families; my sister-in-law Anna Marie—who is like a sister to me—and her family. Each also deeply connected to Bill, I see and hear him in them, and it balms my spirit and warms my heart.

To Jan Richardson, Carol McDonald, Julie Blythe, Joy Haning, Helen Swaar, and Patty Noonan: Even as you walked your own labyrinths of grief and loss, you opened your arms and your hearts to companion me on mine. I give thanks for you each day.

To Vicki, Mickey and Nile, Jeanne and Terry, Jim and Sandy: Your friendship and love, your companionship and encouragement have grounded, helped, and kept me in ways you will never know. Simply by being part of my life, you bless me, and I am grateful for you.

My amazing editorial team made this huge and tender undertaking as easy and life-giving as it could possibly be. Not just my editor but also my friend, Christianne Squires's keen eye and expert guidance helped me turn this alphabet soup of emotion into a coherent volume, caring not only for my words and the book they would become, but also my heart, my soul, my spirit, and my faith. Ines Monnet, Callie Walker, Susanne Clark, and Hannah Bauman turned the final manuscript into a creation that is not only eminently readable, but beautiful and accessible, and blessed me as they did so.

Members of the Light House online community helped immeasurably, companioning me with empathy and grace, selflessly sharing their wisdom, expertise, guidance, and compassionate presence. I am particularly grateful to Examen Group 2: Leanne Shawler, Sandra Logan, Beth Knight, Debbie Huff, Jenny Pace, Emily Ball, Cindy Van Lunen, and Katy Allen, who hold space with and for me each week.

Walking both the labyrinth of grief and loss and the writer's path with me, the members of the Bookwifery Collective have been invaluable companions without whom this book would not exist. To

Jen Willhoite, Cindy Van Lunen, Jean Lovell, Kathryn Coneway, Melynne Rust, Janice Gutierrez, Lisa Degrenia, Anne Brock, Jenny Gehman, and Becky Grisell: You see me, you hear me, you get me, and you lavish me with encouragement, support, and love.

I am deeply grateful to and for my spiritual director, Trudy Rankin, who—among her many wise insights—first noticed the labyrinth theme emerging from the book and shared not only her intuition but her beautiful Chartres hand labyrinth with me.

And many thanks to my local writing group, Writers 4 All Seasons. Your careful listening and your precise yet constructive and kindly offered critique have made me a better writer and this a better book.

ABOUT THE AUTHOR

Kathy Swaar served the Presbyterian Church (USA) as a Commissioned Lay Pastor for twenty-five years, over eighteen of those as a solo pastor.

After receiving her MA in Child, Family, and Community Services (a social-work style program) from the University of Illinois Springfield, Kathy served UIS as an adjunct assistant professor, teaching communications and helping skills courses for the Criminal Justice program for ten years.

As president and CEO of W-K Swaar Enterprises, Inc., Kathy currently oversees the management of her family's central Illinois grain farm. A full-time writer since 2015, she resides in central Florida.

Follow her on Instagram at @kathy_swaar, on Facebook at www.facebook.com/KathySwaarAuthor, and on her website at www.kathyswaar.com.

Made in the USA
Las Vegas, NV
17 February 2021

18091757R00089